To Martin and Helena
we do hope you will
enjoy this touch of Spain

The
Buenvino
Cookbook

Recipes from our farmhouse in Spain

Sam and Jeannie

We were formally created "Sons and Daughters of Los Marines" by the town hall a few years ago, and we would like to dedicate this book to the people of Los Marines with our profound gratitude for their warmth and generosity to us, and for welcoming us into their community.

Como hijos adoptivos de La Villa de Los Marines, nos gustaría dedicar este libro a su gente tan entrañable, nuestros Marineros, con nuestra más sincera gratitud por su generosidad hacia nosotros y por habernos acogido tan bien en su comunidad.

Photography by Tim Clinch

The Buenvino Cookbook

Recipes from our farmhouse in Spain

Jeannie and Sam Chesterton

BFP

Foreword

Darina Allen

Every now and then I come across a really special place, a gem so out of the ordinary that I have mixed feelings about revealing its whereabouts. Pink-washed Finca Buenvino emerges out of the oak and chestnut woods at the end of a winding country avenue, in the middle of the Sierra de Aracena nature reserve in Andalusia, Spain.

The view across the hills, thickly wooded with sweet chestnut and cork oak, is spectacular; here and there are olive groves, walnut trees and orchards of plums, peaches and figs. Wild rocky escarpments are covered in cistus and tree heathers. Stone walled mule tracks meander from village to hamlet, perfect for walking or riding.

The place itself is magical, but it is Jeannie's cooking which sets the seal on a perfect visit. Over the years she has honed her approach to the cooking of Spain, giving many dishes her own special twist. She uses home-grown organic vegetables from the orchards at the bottom of the Buenvino valley, and good organic beef which is raised locally at the Dehesa de San Francisco. She serves fabulous Spanish cheeses, too: Cabrales, Manchego, a creamy melting Torta wrapped in its traditional band of lace, and the famous Tetilla from Galicia, as well as great local Aracena goat's cheese from Monte Robledo.

It's impossible to talk of Aracena without mentioning the local star ingredient: Iberian pork. This local breed is famous for the *jamón ibérico* which is created from it, but the fresh pork itself is outstanding – a red meat akin to beef – and Jeannie excels in its preparation.

For me, the whole experience of staying at Finca Buenvino was even more exciting because I could at last learn first hand about the rearing of the famous black pigs and the production of pata negra, Iberian acorn-fed ham, the finest cured ham in the world. The village of Jabugo, famous for the production of jamón, is just a few miles away from Buenvino, but there was no need to venture that far because Sam and Jeannie's own pigs were gorging themselves on the acorns under the cork oaks. Sam cures the delicious hams himself, slowly and painstakingly, in the time-honoured way.

We ate slivers of jamón for tapas every evening, never tiring of the exquisite flavour and extraordinary silken and melting texture of the meat and fat. Jeannie also served fried salted almonds, delicious Aracena potato crisps, and little fresh anchovies pickled with garlic and parsley, or else a small dish of clams and beans; something different every evening... And then we would go in to dinner!

If you don your walking boots, you can set out across the hills to Linares de la Sierra, a little village with narrow cobbled streets and patterned stone 'mats' outside every house. In the central square the village ladies wash their clothes in a communal well, chatting contentedly in a wonderfully relaxed and convivial way, maybe not everyone's cup of tea, but infinitely more sociable than flinging the laundry into the washing machine. There, we had a delicious simple lunch at the local Los Arrieros restaurant. Several memorable dishes included *hígado aliñado*, very thin slices of Iberian pig's liver cooked with sweated onion and extra virgin olive oil and served cold, dressed with vinaigrette and coriander leaves. It's a typically local dish, which Jeannie often serves, and the recipe is within these pages. Tiny vol au vents came to the table, filled with black pudding mousse and fresh mint, followed by succulent pig's trotters, then grilled local goat's cheese on toast, served with honey and oregano (the latter you will also find in this book).

On another day, we did a six-hour walk through the breathtakingly beautiful terrain just north of Buenvino. We stopped for a lunch of jamón, salchichón, and local cheese in the village pub in Cortelazor. This part of rural Spain is totally unspoilt, the people are friendly and welcoming, the food honest and delicious.

We eagerly looked forward to every meal in the area and at Buenvino itself – Jeannie is a wonderful cook – and here she shares her recipes, which I know you will enjoy as much as I have.

Darina Allen

DARINA ALLEN is founder of the world-famous Ballymaloe Cookery School in County Cork, Ireland.

Introduction

Jeannie Chesterton

Finca Buenvino, home to our family for almost 30 years, lies at the heart of the natural park of the Sierra de Aracena, one of the most beautiful parts of Andalusia.

The house sits on a hill forested with chestnut trees and cork oaks. In the valley below are olive groves and fruit orchards. Nearby lies the *dehesa*; rolling park-like country which is home both to the black Iberian pigs that provide delicious jamón, salchichón and morcilla, and to the magnificent red Retinto cattle that are renowned for their beef.

A few times a year, I run cookery courses for small groups. My personal take on Spanish and Mediterranean cooking incorporates the pounded picadas of Catalonia – a mixture of garlic, bread, spices or even chocolate added to a dish at the end of cooking – as well as the use of fruit and spices in savoury dishes that is so typical both of Andalusia and of the Maghreb. We use fresh local ingredients: Iberian pork, mountain lamb and wild venison and boar. Fish comes mainly from the Huelva coast. We have eggs from our Violet Andalusian hens. We kill and cure our own jamón ibérico and bake fresh wholemeal loaves and Moroccan flatbreads from organic flour shipped down from Albacete. Honey comes from the hives above the orchards, organic vegetables and herbs from the garden. In autumn, wild mushrooms spring up in the woods, while just-picked chestnuts from the forest below the house, roasted in the open fire, are perfect with a glass of rich, dry Chesterton oloroso straight from the barrel which sits in the conservatory. This was a gift from a dear friend and is blended for us in the Gonzalez Byass bodega.

Although my cooking is influenced by Spanish ingredients and methods, this is not a thoroughbred Spanish cookbook, of which there are many. Instead, it's a reflection of our way of life and the food we share with our guests.

Stairs up from the meadow below the house

Country life then and now: the changes over 30 years

Sam Chesterton

When Jeannie agreed to marry me, I was already spending time in Spain, living in an outbuilding on a friend's hacienda in the hills above Seville. The initial plan to spend a summer away from London had become a more permanent commitment almost before I had realised. I had grown to love the hills of the Sierra Morena, with their brilliant light and clean, sharp air scented with pine, eucalyptus, and rosemary.

It was brave of Jeannie to take me on; but even braver to agree to come from London to my small converted stable which was not only without electricity but had a bad habit, after dark, of ceasing to provide water from the taps. This then required a long, spooky walk down to the pump house, then a tussle, tugging on a rope, to start an obstreperous diesel engine. But we had talked it over and, after working together at shooting lodges in Scotland, we knew we wanted to open a country guest house.

Finca Buenvino lies about a kilometre outside the village of Los Marines; 'our village' we call it... it's also our family, in a way. It's where our children started school, and it's where we do much of our socialising today. A few years ago we were given the agreeable surprise of being formally adopted by the town hall and we have a certificate to prove that we are *Hijos Adoptivos de la Villa de Los Marines*.

Eduardo, who used to help us out at the farm and with guests, had been our first employee. A truckload of tiles had arrived one September afternoon, about nine months after we had acquired the farm. We needed to get the whole lot of them stacked on the ground, in readiness for the day that we would have a house. We had not even started building then, but were going through the elaborate dance of gaining planning permission. Not knowing the village at all, Jeannie and I drove in and went into the first tiny bar we saw, to ask if anyone knew someone who would be able to come and give us a hand with unloading the truck.

We'd not even understood that the weekend before had been Los Marines' fiesta, several nights of dancing and drinking, and one day of recuperation on what was known as *el día de la resaca*, hangover day.

Of course we had chosen hangover day to cruise into town looking for a willing worker! Felicidad was behind the bar, and she came out immediately, 'I've someone for you; just wait!' She crossed the street into her house and hauled her son Eduardo out of bed. He arrived, rubbing his eyes but enthusiastic, and went down the road to fetch his friend Gonzalo. Soon, Eduardo and Gonzalo were working for us, clearing scrub and putting in the first ditches that would eventually hold foundations and drains. Gonzalo managed to do himself some damage with a pickaxe when he hauled it out of a hole where it had become jammed, and the handle flew back and clunked him on the forehead.

A month later, Jeannie and I drove with the pair of them to Lisbon for a weekend. Neither of them had been to another country before, so everything was exciting and new. 'Esto es Hollywood!' exclaimed Eduardo when he jumped out of the car.

Clockwise from top left: Luciano and Felicidad, who fed our children lunch every day during their school years; carnations on a Los Marines balcony; horses off to the blacksmith in Los Marines; La Fuentecilla (the little fountain) in Los Marines

Eduardo was still with us once the foundations were in and the house was going up. Our eldest son Jago had started to walk by then, and his chief amusement was to play in the piles of builder's sand, or waddle around behind Eduardo, who he worshipped, clutching a pair of pliers. This earned him the early nickname of *Alicate* ('pliers').

When the house was opened for business, Eduardo came in to help us with dinner in the evenings. He would don the stiff white jacket with brass buttons which had been given to him during his military service, when he had waited at table in the officers' mess in Jerez. International guests would gather in the drawing room for drinks and tapas, then, suddenly, the doors would burst open and Eduardo would bound in, announcing, 'Dinner is soft!' We soon decided this was an unnecessary touch of theatre... Rehearsals in the kitchen went like this: Me, 'Dinner is served.' Eduardo, 'Dinner is soft.' 'No, served.' '...saved?' There is no 'urr' sound in Spanish, of course.

Eduardo and his fiancée Amparo came to Scotland with us, and we took them down to London. It was the first time either of them had been on a plane.

Naturally, when Jago started school at the age of four, Feli, Eduardo's mother, kindly offered to give him lunch so that we would not have to drive in and out of the village, then back in the afternoons for late school. All our children ended up lunching with Feli on weekdays, along with her own grandchildren (Eduardo's niece and nephew), and other cousins. They usually had a *puchero* of some kind; generally a ham bone boiled up with chickpeas, vegetables and pieces of chorizo or black pudding. '*¡Come Niño!*' Feli would cry if there was too much ragging going on. 'Eat up child!'

Clockwise from top left: Looking out at the front courtyard at Finca Buenvino; the front courtyard; entrance arch to the courtyard; roses and wisteria on the east side of the house

There was always plenty of bread to go with the meal, as Feli ran the local bread distribution from her front hall. There was no bakery in such a small community (population 300) and bread was delivered from Aracena, a 10-minute drive away. Our post was also delivered to her house as there is no post office. Now it goes to a letterbox which the village policeman kindly screwed to the wall for us in the town hall.

The good road which passes our gates on its way to Lisbon from Seville was then single-tracked with many bends. Traffic was scarce, and it was a sobering experience whenever we encountered a towering and overloaded cork lorry, coming head-on at us on some blind corner; a game of chicken was out of the question, and we would find ourselves driving into the straw-coloured undergrowth, our engine stalling as the truck faded dustily into the distance behind us.

Each night, the frontier with Portugal was closed from 10pm until 6am. Before the advent of the EU and the central planning of new international roads, Aracena and the Baixo Alentejo over the border were but two forgotten corners of two nations, where two peasant cultures rubbed shoulders slightly uncomfortably. Both nations regarded one another with vestigial suspicion and, in the early 1980s, during the Falklands war, Spain would transmit the news from the Buenos Aires Generals' point of view, while Portugal was rooting for Blighty. Crossing the border by car involved a 45-minute stop. Kepis, jack boots and the smell of black tobacco smoke took one back to an earlier time, when crossing the border was a serious affair.

In the frontier Spanish town, Rosal, there were shops selling tourist treasures such as brandy bottles in the shape of a flamenco dancer. People would venture to the Portuguese side to buy coffee, Elvas plums or linen, but these were private bus excursions, or adventurous individuals going it alone. There were no large trucks travelling through the night – as there are now – with flowers grown in Cádiz destined for the markets of Lisbon.

Coffee from Portugal has always been preferred here since the days of the Civil War, when it was scarce in Spain. With Portugal's former colony Brazil being a major producer, a trade of smuggling coffee had grown up in the hills of La Contienda, the much fought-over area just west of us which changed hands several times over the centuries (hence its name, almost 'the bone of contention').

Slamming the border shut at night seemed logical in those days, so there was utter silence for us on the farm, but for the braying of an ass in the valley below or the hoot or shriek of an owl from the forest. The great dark sky over our heads was scattered with bright stars, which today are slightly dimmed on the horizon by faint light pollution. But we are lucky, we can still sit on our terrace and watch the shooting stars fall silently into the August night, or count satellites as they travel relentlessly. We can hear the tinkle of the goats' bells on the far hill, the bark of a fox, and yes, the donkey too.

What else has changed? The beautiful cast-iron market building in Aracena, our local town, has long since gone. It was designed in the early 20th century by Anibal Gonzalez, the famous architect of the Plaza de España in Seville. It's been replaced by something anodyne, but which fitted in with the new rules of the European Union. In the early 1980s the market was a hive of activity, where smallholders of the area would bring vegetables and fruit, or buckets of milk and baskets of eggs. Large zinc bowls held chickpeas that had been soaked overnight, ready to be boiled up, while on the butchers' stalls it was still common to see the flayed head of a goat staring blankly ahead.

EU bureaucracy, improved transport and refrigeration have done away with the picturesque and bustling market. Elderly stallholders, confused by the introduction of VAT and new health rules, took early retirement rather than having to confront the hassle of incomprehensible paperwork. Nowadays, uniform vegetables come to the new supermarkets on huge trucks along the wide new roads, but we are lucky because the smallholders of the area, many of them friends, still arrive at our door with gifts of tomatoes, aubergines or courgettes when they have a glut, while we in turn will bring them gifts from our own over-production, a basket of figs perhaps, or a sack of potatoes.

At first glance it seems strange that this deeply rural corner of Spain should so utterly have abandoned the market culture which is still alive in much of the rest of the country. On closer inspection there is logic behind the apparent contradiction, and it explains why the best food markets are to be found in the cities rather than in the small country towns and villages. There are two reasons for this. Firstly, the population is concentrated in the cities, so farm produce gravitates to urban markets. Secondly, and perhaps more importantly, rural Spain (certainly Andalusia) is principally composed of big *latifundio* estates which make for vast areas of monoculture. Country people in these endless olive groves, or wide horizons of sunflowers, or cotton, have to grow their own alternatives if they are lucky enough to own a small *huerta*, or, if they are *jornaleros* (day workers on the huge farms owned by the aristocracy and big business) they may well not own any land, and must rely on middlemen to bring supplies from the central city markets to the small shops in their rural towns. The people of Lepe cannot live on strawberries alone, even if they have become millionaires from the cultivation of them.

One of the great attractions of the Sierra de Aracena is that it consists of *minifundio* (smallholdings). This means that most families have an acre or less of olive grove, an orchard and a chestnut wood; somewhere to raise a pig and grow vegetables, or start a small business growing tuberoses. If they don't own an orchard, their cousin does. It is particularly useful when there is an economic crisis, as there is now, because families can look after themselves to a great extent. This naturally makes for happier people, and happier people tend to be more welcoming and social creatures.

Spain has always been quick to embrace progress, sometimes overlooking the good things which might have been held on to, even as the country stepped eagerly into the modern world. To counter this encroaching supermarket culture, young people with an alternative view of life – often former city dwellers who have come to the countryside to find honest food and a simpler way of being – have tried from time to time to set up farmers' markets to promote artisan foods, cheeses and honeys and home-grown produce. It's not always been successful, but times are changing. A new organic shop in Aracena bucks the trend and is slowly having more success. Another farmers' market initiative starts in a few days, even as I write.

At Finca Buenvino we try to be part of this progressive-regressive movement. We believe that good simple food and honestly produced ingredients are the way forward. By all means let us sing the praises of mains water and drains, effective refrigeration, better lighting and improved transport, but let us not lose sight of what was good in the past and what can still be recovered of that simplicity.

Top right: Breakfast in the dining room; Bottom right: dinner in the kitchen courtyard

How I learned to love Spanish food

Jeannie Chesterton

Much of the food in my book is Spanish country fare that uses local produce and which, at first glance, might seem rough and ready. On closer examination it is subtly engaging, with an almost medieval use of spices. On the whole, these dishes are easy to prepare in advance and can be kept warm or hot until it is time to dine. This gives me time to change out of my apron and join my guests for a drink before dinner.

When I discovered cooking, it was like a window opening for me on to a new world. Undiagnosed throughout my school days as dyslexic, I had become resigned to coming bottom of the class and had almost concluded that I was no good at anything.

I had cooked a little at home, then, in my late teens, I trained at the Cordon Bleu School in London. The style of the school in the early 1960s – with its reliance on cream and butter – has gone out of fashion in some respects, but the course offered me a foundation on which to build. Over my early years in the kitchen I began to understand the ways in which ingredients reacted with each other, how important was the balance of acidity and sweetness, how to taste for seasoning... the basics. Cooking is an art and I learned how to 'paint' with good ingredients, how to use spices and herbs and how to adjust traditional recipes and improve upon them, or alter them subtly.

In the 1960s and 1970s my cooking work took me to shooting lodges in the Scottish Highlands, bars and restaurants in Edinburgh and far-flung Hong Kong, private chalets in the Austrian Alps, and for many years into the catering kitchens of *By Word of Mouth* in London.

When I married Sam in the early 1980s and came to deep rural Spain, it was a country unknown to me. I was at first disappointed by the sometimes indifferent – or, frankly, bad – food we were served. Too often there were no vegetables on the plate, or if there were they came from a can. The selection of sweets was limited to rice pudding or canned peaches. Meat was often over-salted (and often still is); fish was sometimes cooked rigid.

When we were engaged and on my first drive south through the sweltering July landscape of central Spain, we stopped in the middle of Castile, at the top of a mountain pass, and we had a meal of fermenting (literally fizzy) chickpea soup and a tough piece of grey beef, followed by grapes and manchego cheese which sweated and wriggled across the dish since it was alive with maggots! Sam did not wish to give offence and insisted we eat enough soup to be able to see the pattern at the bottom of the plate. It was a hot afternoon, the inn was small and dilapidated and the woman who gave us lunch, such as it was, was elderly and had made do with what she could find. We struggled through it all (we were hungry!) and enjoyed the grapes. We survived.

It was not until I had spent a few days at Sam's small house in the mountains north of Seville that I discovered there was good food to be had in Spain, if you knew where to look. We sampled Manolo's delicous tapas at the Bar Los Mellis in Cazalla de la Sierra: *gambas al ajillo*; hot, crisply fried fresh anchovies; eggs and spicy chard.

Clockwise from top left: Jeannie with chives; Sam, our daughter Grania and Jeannie; Sam eating lunch; Mariano Sanchez, who sometimes ploughs the farm, enjoying a beer

Our landlords introduced us to the La Dorada restaurant in Seville, where waiters in blue blazers darted in and out of swing doors, the décor was reminiscent of some smart yacht, and the fish jumped straight out of the sea on to our plates. Here we tucked in to *lubina a la sal* and roasted pepper salad; huge grilled *cigalas* and garlic mayonnaise; cos lettuce hearts served with toasted garlic and *pimientos del piquillo*... there was hope after all.

We started to hunt straight away for an old house which we could convert into a guest house; but while Sam fell in love with – and thought it feasible to buy – a 16th-century hacienda, miles from anywhere, with no electricity (but yes, it did have a steam-driven olive press!), I was more practical. Where would I shop? If we were lucky enough to have children, where would they go to school? Sam's favourites were all 40 minutes from the nearest urban centre and I could see myself slowly going mad with the eternal white washing, the daily hour and a half spent in a car, no guests and no income.

Friends from Seville introduced us to the Sierra de Aracena, further west. The houses were small. Too small to be guest houses. At last we found a beautiful forested hill, and Sam had a vision. 'We'll build here,' he said, as I stared at the scrubby hillside and overgrown forest. We had never before considered building, but we followed our instincts; the place felt magical, and it felt right. There was a view to die for. There was a stream filled with primroses. There was a spring, there was a road nearby. There was a charming market town not far away, there was a bewitching village and there were friendly people. It looked as though there would eventually be a possibility of mains electricity and a telephone line.

Our children. Clockwise from top left: Jago helping himself to lunch; Grania; lunch al fresco; Charlie putting his bread out to prove

While waiting for planning permission, we travelled in Spain and Portugal looking for old building materials, visited brick factories in Seville, spent nights in Lisbon, travelled up through Madrid where we bought old reclaimed panels for doors and walls and passed through Barcelona on our way to the United Kingdom, to spend time with family and friends.

It took us three years in all, from finding the spot to building the house and opening for guests. I was instantly happy in my new kitchen. I'd spent the last few years either travelling, or cobbling things together on a small gas ring in our nearby rented village house. Now I was itching to get going with the fresh ideas that were brimming in my head. I loved the special genius of Catalan food, with its picadas and sauces, so different from the heavy, creamy French cooking of my training; in Andalusia I appreciated the simplicity of the food, with the combination of spices half-Moroccan and half-local, such as cumin and lemon, or the rabbit with cloves which we were served for dinner at a friend's home.

I embraced different ideas of savoury and sweet combinations: chocolate and salt; or the Italian combination of black figs sprinkled with salt and ground black pepper, then anointed with olive oil and lemon juice. A magical marriage.

I'd always thought how lovely it would be to have a lemon tree just outside the kitchen, so I could rush out and pick one for my gin and tonic in the evening when I was slaving over a hot stove, or gather basketfuls to make lemon curd or marmalade. Alas, it was never to be. We live above the lemon line, if there is such a thing.

This book is my take on cooking in southern Europe, with an emphasis on Iberia. Some of it may not be authentic, but it is all damn good, and although I do use a little butter and cream in some of my recipes (because it cannot be substituted), it is healthy.

The recipes

Picadas and pestos

Mortar and pestle vs food processor

The picada of Catalonia, the pesto of Genoa, the tarator of the Middle East and the majada (or, colloquially, majá) of Andalusia all come from the same idea: a mixture of nuts, seeds, herbs and spices, ground in a mortar and pestle, sometimes with breadcrumbs or fried bread added, used to thicken and flavour stocks and sauces in stews and tagines, or to be turned into soups or sauces themselves.

Although not strictly authentic, we tend to use a food processor when making large quantities of Pesto Genovese or Sun-dried tomato pesto (see pages 31 and 33). We also use it for Gazpacho and Ajo blanco (see pages 70 and 72), as do most Andalusians nowadays, even though these soups were originally made slowly in a mortar.

When we first came to this part of Andalusia I watched a friend of ours, a builder, who was working on a remote farm, preparing lunch for his fellow workers. Salt, garlic, stale bread, green peppers, cucumber and tomatoes were

Clockwise from top left: Our romesco; Alioli and Quince alioli (see pages 30 and 32)

added in turn to a rough cork bowl and pummelled with the flat, rounded end of a wooden spoon-cum-pestle, before the addition of cool spring water. (These irregular cork bowls, prized objects, grow naturally over the wounds in a tree from a severed branch.) Olive oil and vinegar were carried in a pair of hollowed-out cow's horns, with cork bases and stoppers.

It is good to know that shepherds and goatherds still make their lunch this way – in isolated huts and farmhouses down on the great estates of the plains or in the remote cork-forested sierras or high pastures of the *transhumancia* – but nowadays, many people in our Aracena mountains have a car or a motorbike. Smallholdings (*minifundio*) are the norm here, and workers can return to their homes at night in their villages. Each morning they make, or are made, a *gazpachito*, using a hand-held blender, and they take the cold soup out in a flask to the field or forest.

For the smaller quantities used in the preparation of a subtle picada or majá, the mortar is vital. It cannot be subsituted. We use a large heavy marble mortar from the Sierra de Granada with a wooden pestle. We also have a smaller stoneware mortar with a stoneware-tipped pestle for lesser quantities of spices and herbs. A small coffee grinder is also good for this, though oils from herbs such as rosemary can eat into any plastic casing. Stone mortars are resistant to this form of corrosion and, anyway, there is something satisfying about grinding spices finely in the mortar.

Making and using a picada

The most usual picada of Catalonia is a mixture of garlic, parsley, pine nuts, fried bread and almonds, ground into a coarse paste, mixed with some of the juices of a fish or meat stew, then returned to the dish for the last 10 minutes or so of cooking. There are many variations and many dishes which benefit from its use. Toasted hazelnuts add richness to a *suquet* or stew of scorpion fish or other rock fish. Fried bread acts as a thickener, while raw almonds give a marzipan tang. A picada of nuts, garlic, parsley and chocolate perfects a dish of venison, beef or boar.

A picada fills out the gaps in a dish, making it complete. Salted anchovies, rinsed and pounded with pine nuts, saffron, sun-dried tomato and fried bread gives an added dimension to a dish of clams, tomatoes and butter beans. In Morocco, a cooked chicken liver is pounded up and added to a chicken and lemon tagine, just as a cod or monkfish liver is pounded in a mortar with the rest of the picada ingredients to add to a fish dish in Catalonia.

At Finca Buenvino we sometimes use a picada in an unorthodox way in our *cocidos*, thick winter country stews of chickpeas and pork, or beans and duck. Parsley and almonds, paprika, cloves or saffron are pounded up with some of the cooked chickpeas from the dish, then mixed with some of the liquid and returned to the pan.

Have fun altering any of the sauced meat or fish recipes in my book by adding the picada of your choice. You will soon find out which you like best, and come up with your own mixtures. Here are some of our favourites.

Our smaller mortar and stomeware-tipped pestle, being used to make a Classic Catalan picada (see overleaf)

Classic Catalan picada

enough to flavour a stew for 6–8

a few saffron strands

sea salt

6 almonds

6 hazelnuts

4 garlic cloves

6 pine nuts

a few sprigs of parsley, chopped

This would go into any braise; for example into a dish of potatoes stewed with pork ribs, or braised quails, or a fish stew. Towards the end of the cooking time, the picada is mixed with some of the cooking juices, ready to be added to the pot. When there are just five or 10 minutes to go, add the picada to the sauce over a low heat and allow to simmer.

❋ First toast the saffron in a dry pan. Grind it in a mortar with a pinch of salt.

❋ Toast the almonds and hazelnuts in the dry pan, tip on to a plate and allow to cool. Add them to the mortar with the garlic, pine nuts and parsley and grind to a coarse paste.

Andalusian majá

enough for 6–8 servings of fish or meat

2 garlic cloves

pinch of sea salt

6 almonds

½ slice of dampened stale white country bread, crusts removed

good bunch of flat-leaf parsley, chopped

5 tbsp extra virgin olive oil

The most simple picada, this one is for garlic lovers only. You can either spoon it directly on to fish or meat before putting it under the grill, to make a tasty garlic crust, or put it into a sauce boat with a squeeze of lemon juice and spoon it over grilled fish or meat.

❋ Grind everything except the oil into a paste, in the order suggested, then stir in the oil.

Classic Catalan picada

THE BUENVINO COOKBOOK

Coriander picada

enough to flavour a stew for 4–6

24 coriander seeds

3 garlic cloves

6 almonds

½ slice of stale white country bread, crusts removed

4 tbsp olive oil

1½ tbsp pine nuts

2–3 sprigs of coriander, chopped

2–3 sprigs of parsley, chopped

You won't find coriander leaves in general use in any other part of Andalusia but, where we live, bunches of them are always on display in the small vegetable shops or in local markets.

In taste, this picada is a little frontier-straddling, falling somewhere between the Algarve, the Alentejo and our own Spanish province. Coriander leaves are in much commoner use over the border, but have traditionally been used in this corner of Huelva province for many years; possibly the taste for it arrived with intermarriage, or because of the historically ill-defined frontier with Portugal.

This picada is excellent and should be to hand in jars and ready to go, to pop into fish dishes.

❋ Sauté the coriander seeds in a dry frying pan until a shade darker and aromatic (watch them carefully as they burn quickly). Tip into a mortar and pound.

❋ Now, each in turn, fry the garlic, the almonds and the bread in oil until golden.

❋ Pound all the ingredients in the mortar, in the order suggested, and add some of the juices from a fish dish (this is especially good with Clams marinière, see page 98), then stir it all back into the pan. It converts the dish into something altogether heartier.

Picada for fish with tomato

enough to flavour a stew for 4–6

a few saffron strands

6 roasted almonds

1 garlic clove

splash of red wine

Like the above picada, this contains no salt. Add to fish and tomato dishes, which themselves are cooked with some salt.

❋ First toast the saffron in a dry pan.

❋ Tip into the mortar with all the other ingredients and grind to a coarse paste.

❋ Add to a dish of Baked octopus and potatoes (see page 94) a few minutes before the end of cooking.

Má de morter

enough to flavour a stew for 6–8

4 garlic cloves, finely sliced

4 tbsp olive oil

4 dried ñora peppers

4 slices of stale white country
bread, crusts removed

6 black peppercorns

One of the oldest and simplest picadas, the name of this literally
means 'that which has been pounded in a mortar'. This is served
with wild rabbit, or is excellent in a dish of tender white beans.

✳ Fry the garlic in the oil until golden, then set the cloves aside.

✳ Fry the peppers in the same oil, then set aside with the garlic.

✳ Now fry the slices of bread until lightly coloured, and lightly fry
the peppercorns, too.

✳ Bash up all the fried ingredients in a mortar, starting with the
garlic, then the peppercorns, followed by the ñora peppers and,
finally, the bread.

Picada for game and red meat

enough to flavour a stew for 6–8

1 slice of stale white country
bread, crusts removed

olive oil

6 almonds

6 hazelnuts

good pinch of sea salt

pinch of ground cloves

4 garlic cloves, roasted
(see page 30)

4 sprigs of parsley, chopped

5g (⅛oz) grated dark chocolate
(75 per cent cocoa solids)

Add to any venison, wild boar or beef casserole and return the
covered dish to the oven or hob for 15 minutes before serving.

✳ Fry the bread in the oil until golden, then tip into a mortar.

✳ Toast all the nuts in a dry pan until a shade darker and smelling
toasted, then tip on to a plate and leave to cool.

✳ Add the nuts to the bread in the mortar with all the other
ingredients and grind to a paste.

Classic romesco

makes a large bowlful for serving with poultry, fish or grilled vegetables.

4 dried ñora peppers

4 slices of stale white country bread, crusts removed

4 tbsp olive oil

4 garlic cloves, finely sliced

2 ripe tomatoes, deseeded and grated

splash of sherry vinegar

6 roasted almonds

salt and freshly ground black pepper

Last but not least, the classic and most famous of all Catalan picadas, so useful to serve with both fish and meat dishes. This can also be added to stews, or spread on to crostini for a delicious tapa. Our own, somewhat tampered-with, version is overleaf.

✳ First, put the peppers into a bowl, cover with just-boiled water and leave for 10 minutes. Drain, then split open and deseed.

✳ Fry the bread in the olive oil in a pan until golden. Set the bread aside, then fry the garlic until golden too; now add the peppers and tomatoes, return the fried bread and add the vinegar and almonds.

✳ Cook the sauce until the liquid has reduced, then pass the whole through a mouli-légumes or a sieve. Season with salt and pepper and allow to cool.

Our romesco

enough for 12 with grilled or poached fish

2 heads of garlic

3–4 slices of stale white country bread, crusts removed

70g (2½oz) blanched almonds

olive oil

2 large red peppers

6 large tomatoes

salt and freshly ground black pepper

red wine vinegar (optional)

Our version of the famous sauce is delicious and different but highly practical, since we get to use the red peppers from our garden. This recipe makes a good quantity and can be kept in the fridge for a week in a covered bowl, for dipping, cooking, or serving as a sauce. It's incredibly useful.

❋ Preheat the oven to 200ºC/400ºF/gas mark 6. Wrap the garlic heads in foil and roast for one hour. Remove and allow to cool.

❋ Meanwhile, put the ripped-up slices of bread and the almonds in the oven to toast. Check and remove the toasted bread and nuts when they are golden, be careful not to burn them. (If you prefer, you can fry the almonds in a little olive oil, stirring constantly with a wooden spoon until they are a light golden colour.)

❋ In another oven dish, roast the peppers and tomatoes in a little olive oil for about 20 minutes; the tomatoes until soft and the peppers until blistered (peppers take a little longer than tomatoes).

❋ Put the peppers in a plastic or paper bag, or a bowl covered with cling film, and allow to cool. The steam generated will make them easier to peel.

❋ Peel the roasted peppers and roasted tomatoes, squeeze out the garlic cloves from their skins, and put them all into a blender.

❋ Blend until smooth, then slowly add the crumbled bread and toasted almonds. Start pouring on olive oil. You need to reach a stiff-but-grainy mayonnaise texture. Don't forget to season with salt and pepper and a little red wine vinegar, if you wish. Serve cold with poultry, fish or grilled vegetables. Or just about anything else.

Pesto Genovese and its derivatives

The classic mixture of pine nuts, basil, pecorino cheese, garlic and olive oil can be adapted, as can all picadas. The fact that they are no longer 'authentic' (we add almonds and manchego) does not destroy their charm, nor affect their usefulness. Feel free to be unorthodox.

If you are making pesto in quantity to keep, adding garlic is not a good idea; it turns rancid. We top up our jars of pesto with oil and confine them to a cool cellar. A fridge will do. Or you can freeze it in small batches. When the time comes to use this garlic-free pesto as a pasta sauce, gently fry sliced garlic cloves in olive oil until golden and transparent, then toss them into pasta with the green sauce.

Here is a recipe for immediate use. We generally use the food processor for this.

enough for 4–6 with pasta

2 garlic cloves

1 tsp sea salt

12 blanched almonds

25g (1oz) pine nuts

leaves from 1 good bunch of basil

60g (2oz) mature manchego cheese, grated

100–150ml (3½–5fl oz) olive oil

❋ Start adding the dry ingredients to a food processor (the small bowl, or a mini food processor, is good for this): the garlic, salt, almonds and pine nuts. Now add the basil and finally the cheese and a little olive oil. When all is blended, pour in as much of the remaining oil as you want to get the texture you prefer.

❋ When the pasta is cooked, stir 1 tbsp of its cooking water into the pesto before pouring it back over the drained pasta.

Here is a recipe for those who want to use a little elbow grease! This makes a chunkier, more authentic sauce than the uniform result you get if you blend it in a food processor.

❋ If using a mortar and pestle, halve the garlic cloves crossways and start grinding them with the salt. (Put the salt in the mortar first; it stops the garlic cloves from slipping around or shooting off across the kitchen.) An initial bashing can gradually give way to a circular grinding motion.

❋ Break the almonds into the mortar and pound them into the mixture, then the pine nuts. The almonds will yield a little oil and, together with the garlic and pine nuts, you should have a stiffish paste.

cont …

✳Now add the basil leaves a few at a time, incorporating them into the paste with a circular motion. This is easier said than done. Add 1–3 tsp of water at this stage if the mass is too sticky. It will combine with the almonds and pine nuts to make a little 'milk' and stop the mixture sticking to the sides of the pestle. Adding oil will only reduce the friction necessary at this stage to grind the leaves.

✳When everything has amalgamated, work the cheese into the mix. Now start to add the olive oil, stirring constantly to make an emulsion and working the paste and oil together with the pestle or, if you prefer, a wooden spoon. Add as much of the remaining oil as you wish, to reach the consistency you prefer.

Alioli

enough for 4

1 tsp sea salt

2 garlic cloves

1 free-range egg

150ml (5fl oz) light olive oil (or a little more if you wish)

sherry vinegar, to taste (Wisdom and Warter is good, but most sherry houses have their own)

OK, this is not strictly a picada or a pesto, though feel free to make it in a mortar and pestle instead of a food processor if you prefer. Make sure all the ingredients are at room temperature. This is the garlic mayonnaise of Spain and is delicious with most things. Try it with Tiny potato omelettes (see page 38). The fruity quince version (see foot of recipe method) is good with grilled poultry or with cold, leftover roast lamb.

✳Put the salt, garlic and egg in the small bowl of a food processor, or in a mini food processor, and switch it on. Once the ingredients are amalgamated, pour in the olive oil, slowly and in a thin stream, at a rate of about 3–4 tbsp at a time. Keep watching. Add more when you think all is integrated. The mixture will gradually emulsify. You can safely add up to about 200ml (7fl oz) of oil, if you want.

✳When the mixture has thickened, add vinegar to taste. Cover and chill until ready to serve.

✳For a quince version, soften 2 tbsp of Quince cheese (see page 210) in a little warm water, then beat it into the mayonnaise.

Sun-dried tomato pesto

enough for 4–6 with pasta

4–5 discs of Sun-dried tomatoes (see page 214), or shop-bought, those labelled 'sun-blush' are softer

25g (1oz) pine nuts

a little oil from the tomato jar

We make this in a food processor, since sun-dried tomatoes can be tough to work in a mortar. Toss hot pasta in butter with a little of its cooking liquid, add fried slices of garlic if you want, or anchovies or basil... then spoon in this pesto. It is also excellent with our Goat's cheese, aubergine and tomato pesto stacks (see page 41).

✳ Grind everything together in the small bowl of a food processor; adding as much water as required to achieve a stiff but soft paste. (If the tomatoes are still soft, the water won't be needed.)

Tapas

The dilemma, when writing about Spanish food, is to find the right section of the book for your dish: is this a tapa? A starter? Perhaps a main course? Quick tapas can be simplicity itself, barely a recipe, more an idea.

Food in Spain, and specifically in Andalusia, is eaten in quite another less formal way than it is in the rest of Europe, with its structured repasts where starter and soup come at the beginning and pudding and cheese at the end. Often, what has been ordered as a main dish in a restaurant will arrive at the table first, followed by some tapas which the diner has fondly imagined will be their starter, much to the consternation of the foreigner.

Neither is there any of the bother with knife and fork etiquette at the table. An Englishman or a Frenchman might have been taught to work his way through the implements from the outer edge towards those nearest to the plate. In Spain, one set of cutlery will be provided in simpler bars and restaurants and you will hang on to it unless changing from fish to meat, or vice versa.

I have tried to be accurate about quantities and servings in the following recipes... but, as there are usually eight to 12 people on a summer's evening (a mixture of house guests, neighbours, drop-ins and tenants from holiday cottages), gathered on the terrace, sitting around the tapas table and talking over their discoveries of the day or watching the swallows swoop and the dragonflies dart, we tend to do things off the cuff. A handful of this and a slurp of that. I shall try to pin things down for you... Fingers crossed!

A colourful tapas spread in the courtyard

THE BUENVINO COOKBOOK

Egg, cheese and vegetable tapas

Tortilla de patatas
Spanish potato omelette

Serves 8 generously (rather large slices)

4–5 potatoes

2 garlic cloves

1 small sweet white onion, sliced

300ml (½ pint) olive oil, or more to taste

8 free-range eggs

salt and freshly ground black pepper

Unlike a French omelette, folded on to the plate with a filling inside, a Spanish potato omelette is one in which the ingredients are cooked together with the egg, to make a solid cake. This is cut into slices to eat warm or at room temperature with a salad, or into smaller pieces, each pierced with a cocktail stick, to serve with drinks.

You can vary the flavours by using chives, cooked artichokes or spinach. A tortilla is also the perfect vehicle for leftover vegetables, even pasta dishes. (Beat yesterday's spaghetti bolognese into the eggs and you will be making what the Italians call a frittata.)

❋Peel the potatoes and slice them lengthways, then cut in half again once or twice horizontally into rough chunks. Chop the garlic cloves into three or four pieces each.

❋Gently simmer the onion in a non-stick, ovenproof frying pan with the oil until transparent, then tip in the garlic and potatoes. Increase the heat to medium. You are softening rather than frying the potatoes, so don't turn the heat too high or you'll brown them.

✳ Meanwhile, lightly beat the eggs in a bowl and season to taste.

✳ As the potatoes soften and begin to break up, take them out of the pan with a slotted spoon and add them to the eggs. Mix thoroughly and return to the oily pan over a medium heat. The eggs will start to cook from the outside in. Make sure the outer edges are not sticking by passing a palette knife around and lifting the tortilla away from the sides of the pan from time to time.

✳ When the tortilla is almost set, place under a hot grill to finish the middle. (If you are quick and sure of yourself, place a plate over the omelette, but make sure it is bigger than the pan or hot oil will pour over your wrists. Turn it over quickly above the sink, then slide it back into the pan upside down.) The grill is not as messy!

✳ When cooked, turn the omelette on to a plate and serve, warm or at room temperature, sliced like a cake, with a green salad.

Mini tortilla de patatas
Tiny potato omelettes

This a great way to use up cold boiled potato left over from the previous day.

✳ Peel and chop cooked potato finely and place in a bowl with a handful of chopped chives and parsley leaves. Beat 4 free-range eggs with salt and pepper, then pour them over the potatoes. Stir together vigorously; it does not matter if the potatoes break up a little.

✳ Now pour a little oil into a pan and heat gently. Spoon some of the egg and potato mix into the oil. Each tortilla should be about the size of a small pancake or drop scone. Let it cook on one side, then flip.

✳ Place on a warm dish and keep warm in a low oven until you want to serve them. (Don't leave them there more than 20 minutes.) To eat them cold, just leave them to cool, then serve with a little mayonnaise or Alioli (see page 32). Fab!

Artichokes with jamón

Serves 10–12 as part of a mixed tapas, or 4–6 as a starter

6–8 artichokes

lemon juice

olive oil

2 garlic cloves, cracked with the side of a knife

100g (3½oz) jamón Ibérico offcuts, *tacos de jamón* (the drier pieces of a ham which are used for flavouring), or bacon or pancetta lardons

150ml (5fl oz) white wine

salt and freshly ground black pepper

Artichokes are plentiful in Andalusia in late autumn, winter and early spring. Fields of them stretch out beside the Guadalquivir River at Cantillana, not far from Seville, and they are also grown in the plains around Granada. They are pleasingly architectural plants, with decorative grey-green, scrolling leaves. You will always find artichokes in the markets at this time of year, and they are often served braised with carrots, peas, garlic, a little water and olive oil. Here they are the star ingredient.

✳ Remove the tough outer leaves of the artichokes and cut off their tops (making sure the hairy inner 'choke' is completely removed; use a teaspoon to get at it all if you need to) and stems. Put the artichoke hearts into water acidulated with some lemon juice to prevent discoloration.

✳ Put 2–3 tbsp of olive oil into a wide sauté pan and add the garlic. Cook gently until softened, then mash with a fork. Now drain the artichoke hearts, cut them into halves and put them into the garlic and oil, flat side-down, packing them into the pan. Sprinkle the jamón over the artichokes, along with the wine and 300ml (½ pint) of water, so the artichokes are almost covered by the oily liquid. Season with salt and pepper and allow to simmer on a medium-high heat, topping up the liquid when necessary with more water. Cook for 45 minutes, then test to see if they are tender: a cocktail stick should meet no resistance. If they need more cooking, just continue for a little longer.

✳ Remove the artichokes to a warmed dish and reduce the cooking liquid over a high heat until the garlicky sauce thickens. Pour the sauce back over the artichokes and serve with enough forks and bread for the company.

Pimientos de Padrón
Fried Padrón peppers

Serves 8 as part of a mixed tapas
250g (9oz) Padrón peppers
5 tbsp extra virgin olive oil
sea salt, to serve

These small green peppers, originally grown in Galicia around the town of Padrón, just south of Santiago de Compostela, are now more widely cultivated and have become very popular all over the country and further afield.

We know them as Russian roulette: although most of them are sweet, every now and then one will blow your socks off with its heat.

❋ Wash the dust of the fields off the peppers and dry them carefully with a tea towel so they don't spit when you add them to the pan.

❋ Heat the olive oil in a wide pan that has a lid and, when warm, add the peppers. When the oil is hot and the peppers are frying, cover the pan. Allow to cook for two minutes, shaking from time to time. The peppers should not be browned all over, only softened.

❋ Drain on kitchen paper and sprinkle with sea salt to serve.

Goat's cheese, aubergine and tomato pesto stacks

Serves 8 as part of a mixed tapas, or 4 as a starter

16 x 2.5cm circular slices of aubergine (about 3 aubergines)

75ml extra virgin olive oil

salt and freshly ground black pepper

1 quantity Sun-dried tomato pesto (see page 33)

2 courgettes

16 slices of goat's cheese from a log, each about a finger thick

spinach, lamb's lettuce or other salad leaves

2 tsp balsamic vinegar (or a mix of sherry vinegar and sweet Pedro Ximenez)

Aracena has two famous goat's cheeses. One smells so strong that it is sold as *queso pestoso* ('stinking cheese')! However, for this dish we use a milder goat's cheese, either from Ronda or from Extremadura. These cheeses are rolled into the shape of a log and have a similiar texture to some dry French chèvre cheeses.

At the Finca we have goats on our hillside, which we milk in springtime for yogurt and cream cheese. They escaped once too often into the neighbour's vineyard and chewed the tender and irresistible shoots of his vines. A Guardia Civil was called in to witness us identifying the offending animals, which the neighbour had locked into a shed before calling the police. When we reported to the barracks to make a statement the following day, the chief of the Guardia Civil was laughing at our lack of composure. 'Goats are very *very* bad,' he announced, 'unless roasted with lots of garlic, bay leaves and wine; then they are very good indeed!'

We have since fenced off the woodland of the Finca and hope to have a goat-free orchard... and vineyard next door.

❋ Brush the aubergine slices with oil, season lightly and grill for five minutes, turning once. Cool, then spread with the pesto.

❋ Meanwhile, trim the ends from the courgettes and thinly slice lengthways with a vegetable peeler, so you get fine, ribbon-like slices. You will need 16 slices. Blanch the slices in boiling salted water for 30 seconds, then plunge into cold water, then drain.

❋ Preheat the oven to 200ºC/400ºF/Gas 6. Place each slice of cheese on a slice of aubergine and pesto on a baking tray. Top with another slice of aubergine. Cross over two courgette 'ribbons' on top. (For taller stacks to serve as starters, as in the photo, stack two of these parcels of aubergine, pesto and cheese on top of each other before crossing them with the blanched courgette strips.)

❋ Cook in the hot oven for six or seven minutes, then place on a plate with a few leaves. Spoon over the balsamic vinegar, or a mixture of sherry vinegar and sweet Pedro Ximenez wine to serve.

Left: Goat's cheese, aubergine and tomato pesto stacks; Far left: Fried Padrón peppers

Ensalada de higos y queso fresco con jamón y miel
Fig and goat's cheese salad with jamón and honey

*Serves 8 as part of a mixed tapas,
or 4 as a starter*

16 figs

lemon juice

250g (9oz) fresh goat's cheese,
torn or cut into pieces, or
drained mozzarella, or ricotta

16 paper-thin slices of jamón
ibérico, cut into strips

leaves from 2 sprigs of mint,
finely chopped

2 tbsp extra virgin olive oil

1 tbsp sherry vinegar

1 tbsp runny honey

freshly ground black pepper

The fig tree produces two crops most years. First come the *brevas*, long figs which were formed on the bough during the previous autumn; later come the *higos*, much sweeter and plumper, with shorter stems. These are the fruits which formed in the spring.

We serve this dish in August and September when the local *higos* are ripe, or earlier in late June when the *brevas* are ready.

We mostly use fresh goat's cheese (*queso fresco*) but, if you are unable to obtain it, use requesón (cottage cheese), ricotta or mozzarella. Although this is less authentic, it is still delicious.

❀ About 45 minutes before eating, cut the stalks from the figs and quarter them. Place them on a platter. Squeeze a little lemon juice on each section of fig and allow to rest. The lemon juice will permeate the fig and bring out its delicate flavour and colour.

※ Dot the cheese between the figs.

※ Place the slices of jamón over the figs and cheese and sprinkle with the mint.

※ Mix together the oil, vinegar and honey and pour over the figs. Grind some black pepper over the salad and serve.

Tostada de queso fresco con orégano y miel
Toasted goat's cheese with oregano and honey

Serves as many as you want

slices of day-old white country bread, or ciabatta

olive oil

1 garlic clove, halved

sliced fresh goat's cheese, or medium manchego cheese

salt and freshly ground black pepper

dried oregano

runny honey

Many of the local restaurants in the Sierra de Aracena serve a variation of this, using different cheeses, from the fresh goat's cheese to the strong *queso pestoso*. We prefer the version with fresh goat's cheese, pale and soft and with a delicate flavour.

We use day-old bread from the wood-fired baker's oven in Aracena. It's a round loaf and we cut straight across it, cutting the central slices in half as they are too long. You could use ciabatta just as successfully.

※ Preheat the oven to 200°C/400°F/Gas 6. Brush slices of the bread with a little olive oil, then bake them until slightly toasted.

※ Rub the toasts once with the cut side of the garlic, leaving only a ghost-like trace of its fragrance.

※ Cover the toasts from edge to edge with the cheese of your choice. Grind on a little black pepper and sprinkle with salt if the cheese is not salty enough. Place on a baking tray.

※ Return to the hot oven and bake until the cheese has melted and is bubbling. If serving at table as a first course, place each slice on a plate, otherwise, if it is a 'smash-and-grab' tapas session, place the slices on a large dish. Either way, cut through each bread slice with a sharp knife, dividing it into four or five fingers, then push them back together.

※ Sprinkle with dried oregano and pour over pale runny honey (we use rosemary or orange blossom honey). Serve immediately.

Un distraído (literally 'a distracted person')
A distraction

Serves 6–8 as part of a mixed tapas

1–2 large beef tomatoes

slice of pancetta, cut into strips

This is another popular *tapita* in local bars.

❋ Slice the tomatoes thickly and cut each slice in half. Pin a strip of pancetta to each tomato slice with a cocktail stick.

Tomate con orégano
Tomato and oregano

This is a popular summer and autumn snack in the Sierra de Aracena, where oregano grows wild in the woods. It often arrives beside the glass of beer you ordered in a bar at no extra charge; the bar owner probably has his own small vegetable patch, and it's a way of sharing nature's bounty.

Simplicity itself, this is a suggestion rather than a recipe.

❋ Chop two ripe beef tomatoes into chunks. Sprinkle with sea salt and dried oregano leaves. Stick each tomato chunk with a cocktail stick and put them in a saucer or on a side plate. Drizzle with a little extra virgin olive oil. They are ready to go.

Almendras fritas
Fried almonds

Way back in the 1950s, Sam's Irish cousin Tommy Jameson (see right) would eat these almonds from a Waterford crystal bowl lined with the *Cork Examiner* to mop up the oil. Champagne to accompany them, or was it the other way round...?

❋ Take a small pan, add a little olive oil and then shallow-fry some blanched almonds, stirring constantly with a wooden spoon, until they are golden brown all over.

❋ Line a beautiful bowl with some newspaper, put in the almonds and sprinkle with sea salt and freshly toasted cumin seeds.

Cousin Tommy: early memories of olive oil, almonds and lobsters

Cousin Tommy was one of my mother's many cousins in Ireland, where she grew up and where I was born (at the appropriately named Lower Hatch Street Nursing Home, in Dublin). He was great fun and in spite of having undergone a tracheotomy, which meant he could not taste anything properly, insisted on giving his lunch guests fresh lobsters from Ardmore Bay, and home-made mayonnaise made with olive oil. His wonderful cook Agnes Power prepared these in the basement kitchen, where we were sometimes allowed as children. She had bulging bottle-glass spectacles, which made her eyes look enormous, and we were always rather frightened of her as she was quite firm about us staying out of the way.

It always seemed the height of sophistication to me at that time, and still does: roasted almonds; olive oil; lobsters. Tommy knew that my mother had a weakness for lobster, which she had not been allowed as a child, as it was 'far too good for children and only for grown-ups'.

Heaven knows where the olive oil and the almonds came from, possibly from McCarthy's wine vaults in Lismore. It was an old-fashioned purveyor to the Dukes of Devonshire across the road in the castle. In the shop there was a large red coffee grinder, the wonderful smell of coffee, and best of all for us children you could buy strings of brown sugar crystals which looked like the jewellery worn by some 1920s blue stocking from Hampstead. The best fun was to get it home

and smash it with a hammer. Where on earth McCarthy's wine vaults obtained this exotic sugar remains a mystery.

I expect Hugh O'Reilly was responsible for the lobsters. We'd go up to the ruined coastguard station with him at night and sing, 'We're all off to Dublin in the green, in the green.' Even though my mother exhorted us to 'remember who you are!' We were not sure who we were at all.

It was at about this time, in the last years of the 1950s, that a company of which my father was a director bought a wonderful Edwardian Hotel in the south of Spain: the Reina Cristina. We started to alternate summer holidays between there and Ireland. The almonds and the olive oil and the smell of dust and the cork factory in southern Spain became imprinted on my sensory memory along with the damp Irish clifftop walks, the cry of the gulls, the smell of the sea, the cushions of sea pinks and the yellow lichen on the rocks.

When I was 18, I was allowed to spend some weeks with the staff who ran the beach club for the hotel in Spain. I shared a room with Adolfo, who used to look after the deck chairs, the ping-pong table and sun umbrellas and who kept everything spick and span. Every morning I was up early to go off fishing for squid in the bay of Algeciras with the cook, Pepe. Then it would be back to the kitchen for the breakfast – utterly shocking to me at the time – of eggs swimming in olive oil with cloves of garlic. **SC**

A version of Wild asparagus and scrambled eggs 'uncontaminated' by bread, sherry or tomato

Revuelto de espárragos trigueros
Wild asparagus and scrambled eggs

Serves 6–8 as part of a mixed tapas

1 bunch of wild asparagus, or regular asparagus

salt and freshly ground black pepper

2–3 garlic cloves

olive oil

1 slice of stale bread, crusts removed, cut into cubes (optional)

1 tsp fino sherry (optional)

2 tsp tomato purée (optional)

5–8 free-range eggs

The thin wild asparagus plants of the Spanish hedgerow are bitter and astringent, but delicious when prepared carefully. In the UK or Ireland, try to get hold of the thinnest green asparagus you can find in the shops, folklorically known as 'sparrowgrass'.

❃ If using the spiky wild asparagus we have in Spain, cut off the woody stems and bring the soft green parts to the boil in salted water. Throw away the water, fill up with clean cold water and return to the boil. This removes most of the bitterness. Drain the asparagus again, chop it into short lengths and set aside. If using 'tame' cultivated asparagus, cook it in boiling salted water for three to six minutes.

❃ In a small pan, fry the garlic cloves in olive oil with the bread, until the garlic is softened and the bread is golden.

✳ Sprinkle the garlic and bread with the fino sherry, then mash them slightly with the tomato purée. Add the asparagus.

✳ Now break in an egg per person, but no more than eight, even if you are 10 people sharing tapas. Scramble everything together and season with salt and pepper before placing in a serving dish.

Garbanzos
Chickpeas

Canned vs dried and how to deal with the latter

Makes 500g (1lb 2oz) cooked chickpeas

200g (7oz) dried chickpeas

1 tsp bicarbonate of soda

Chickpeas are a standard of Andalusian and Spanish food. You can use them bottled or canned if you are in a rush, or dried if you are happy to give the dish some forethought.

Bottled chickpeas and home-cooked chickpeas are two different creatures. Bottled chickpeas, practical and easy to use, are inferior both in flavour and in texture. It's like comparing the texture of soft fudge with that of macadamia nuts. When you go to the vegetable shops in Aracena you will often see the pulses soaking in a dish.

Here's how to prepare dried chickpeas at home.

✳ The night before you need the chickpeas, put them into a large bowl. Sprinkle the bicarb over the top, then pour on cold water to cover and more. Remember they will swell and you don't want the top layer to dry out, so give them plenty of room. Leave overnight.

✳ In the morning, drain the chickpeas. Put them in a pan with twice their volume of fresh water and bring to the boil. Reduce the temperature to a simmer, cover loosely and cook for an hour. Remove some chickpeas with a slotted spoon and test for texture; they should be tender, but still firm. If they are too hard for your liking, cook for longer, but remember you do not want a mush.

✳ When cooked, drain them in a colander and keep them in an airtight container in the fridge. They will keep for about a week. You can use them in a salad with raw onion and preserved lemons, grind them into houmous, cook them up in a dish of pork or toss into a rice salad. Overleaf is a popular way of using them in Spain.

Espinacas con garbanzos
Spinach with chickpeas

Serves 8 as part of a mixed tapas

1 small sweet white onion, finely sliced (optional)

3 large tbsp olive oil, plus more to thicken

3 garlic cloves, each chopped into 3 or 4, or 1 small garlic clove, crushed

2kg (4lb 8oz) spinach

500g (1lb 2oz) soaked, cooked chickpeas (see page 47)

300ml (½ pint) chicken stock, plus more if needed

2 tsp plain flour

spices to taste (cumin, pepper, cloves); or pinchito spice (see recipe introduction, right)

2 tsp tomato purée (optional)

salt and freshly ground black pepper

Spinach and chickpeas is one of the many Moorish dishes left to Spain. It has many variants, sometimes tomato is introduced, or cumin, or mixed spices such as cloves, cinnamon and black pepper. Another variation adds raisins and pine nuts. Feel free to try any of these. You can also stir in some grated manchego cheese and put the little dishes under the grill to melt the cheese at the last moment before going to table. If you are in a hurry because you have unexpected visitors, you can use a chicken stock cube, canned or bottled chickpeas and frozen spinach. Not the same dish, but tolerably good nevertheless.

The instructions for garlic in the ingredients list are there depending on how you like your garlic. The more you compact a garlic clove the stronger it becomes. Thus a whole cooked garlic clove will be sweet in the mouth, while crushed garlic will taste strongest of all.

Pinchito spice from Granada is a mixture of salt, oregano, caraway, saffron, Indian curry powder, coriander leaf, cumin, anise, cayenne, nutmeg and cloves. It's obtainable in most Andalusian shops. Look out for the packet with the head of an old, bearded wise-looking fellow in a scarlet turban. It's generally used for sprinkling on kebabs 'pinchitos Morunos'.

✳ If using the onion, wilt it in the olive oil. Then, if using chopped garlic, stew it in the olive oil, allowing it to turn golden. If using crushed garlic, just add it to the pan.

✳ Throw in the spinach, stirring, and wilt it down without burning (150ml/5fl oz of water can help at this point, to steam the spinach into submission). Add the chickpeas and half the stock. When all is warmed through, add the remaining stock.

✳ Stir the flour in a little oil in a small bowl to make a runny paste. Take some of the liquid from the spinach and stir it into the paste, then tip back into the spinach and allow to thicken. If it's too thick, add more stock or water; you want a creamy texture.

✳ Add the spices to taste and tomato purée (if using). Season with salt and pepper and serve with thin slices of bread fried in olive oil.

Right: Spinach with chickpeas; Far right: Manchego cheese with candied aubergines or with quince cheese

Queso manchego con berenjenas en almíbar de miel

Manchego cheese with candied aubergines or with quince cheese

✳ Cut a triangle out of a mature manchego cheese. Lay it on its side, and slice off the crusts top and bottom. Now slice your triangular wedge into thin triangles.

✳ Serve either with Aubergines candied in honey or with Quince cheese (see pages 202 and 210).

✳ If using the aubergines, slice them into rounds, leaving the tail on, and reassemble each fruit on the plate with a knife and fork beside it. Your guests can cut the discs in half if they're too big, and arrange on slices of manchego... otherwise you'll have lots of sticky fingers. If using quince cheese, cut it into thin squares or cubes and place one on top of each manchego slice.

Fish tapas

Clams with butter beans

Serves 12–15 as part of a mixed tapas, or 6 as a starter

For the beans

250g (9oz) dried, or 800g (1lb 12oz) canned, butter beans

if using dried beans

a few bay leaves

small handful of peppercorns

For the rest

2 tbsp olive oil, plus more for the beans

4 garlic cloves, sliced

1 sweet onion, finely chopped

2 tomatoes, deseeded and chopped (or grated to save time)

2 bay leaves

100g (3½oz) jamón ibérico offcuts, *tacos de jamón* (the drier pieces of a ham, used for flavouring), or gammon or bacon bits

6 crushed peppercorns

splash of Osborne's Veterano Spanish brandy

700g–1.5kg (1lb 9oz–3lb 5oz) small clams (*almejas*)

100ml (3½fl oz) Tio Pepe fino sherry

salt and freshly ground black pepper

good handful of finely chopped parsley and/or coriander leaves

It's no trouble to soak some beans overnight and cook them up in the morning. You can set them aside until the evening, with a little olive oil poured over them to keep them from drying out or sticking together and a lid on top of the pan. Alternatively, if you forget, or cannot be bothered, open a can or a jar.

Butter beans are used in the mountainous northern province of Asturias in many of the *comidas de cuchara* (literally 'spoon foods', the Spanish term for hearty peasant dishes). Best known is the *fabada*, a stew of butter beans, chorizo and blood sausage, cooked with a ham bone. This recipe is a coastal version, which we serve as a starter, but which can be divided up into small dishes when there is much company, and mingled with other platefuls of pleasure. Serve in small terracotta dishes as a tapa, or in larger soup bowls if it is to be hearty starter. Have some crusty bread on the side to mop up the juices.

If using dried beans

❋ The night before, put the beans in a large bowl, cover with plenty of boiling water and allow to soak overnight.

❋ Next day, drain the beans, put them in a large casserole and add 2.3 litres (4 pints) of cold water, the bay leaves and peppercorns. Bring to the boil slowly over a medium-low heat, then reduce the heat to its lowest and simmer for two hours. The beans will absorb about three times their volume of water. Do not add salt, as it will make them tough. Check occasionally that there is still enough water to cover, adding cold water (not hot) if necessary (local lore says this keeps them tender). Do not stir; they need very gentle treatment to prevent them breaking up. When cooked, drain the beans and set aside. To stop them sticking, pour a little olive oil over them. Keep them warm if you are to use them immediately, or cover and set aside until you are ready, when you will need to warm them through once more.

If using canned beans

✳ Drain and rinse the beans, tip them into a pan and warm them through with a little olive oil.

For the sauce

✳ In another, wide pan heat the 2 tbsp of olive oil and gently fry the garlic and onion. When they turn transparent, add the tomatoes, bay leaves, jamón and peppercorns. Cook for a few minutes, stirring to allow the ingredients to amalgamate. Add the brandy and heat to cook out the alcohol.

✳ Place the clams on top of the mixture, add the fino and cover. Cook gently until the clams have opened (discard any that refuse to open). Tip the contents of the pan on to the warmed-through beans and stir gently. Season to taste with salt and pepper and stir in the herbs just before serving.

Gambas picantes de Marruecos
Moroccan peppered prawns

Serves 8 as part of a mixed tapas

1kg (2lb 4oz) medium-sized
raw frozen tiger prawns
(6–8 per person)

100g (3½oz) unsalted butter

6 garlic cloves, finely chopped

leaves from 1 sprig of parsley,
finely chopped

1 tbsp smoked sweet paprika
(pimientón dulce de la Vera)

¼ tsp smoked hot paprika
(pimientón picante de la Vera)

½ tsp ground cumin

salt and freshly ground
black pepper

lemon wedges, to serve

It is usually simple to get frozen raw prawns in Spain. Most towns have a ready supply of fish, even if they are a long way from the sea. Aracena is no exception and it boasts two fish shops and two market stalls. Unlike most of our recipes, this dish uses butter rather than olive oil.

✽ Allow the prawns to thaw in a colander in the sink, covered with a tea towel to keep flies at bay.

✽ Shell and devein the prawns, remove the heads and leave on the tails. I find it's easier to peel them when they are still slightly frozen.

✽ Melt the butter in a pan over a low heat. Add all the ingredients except the lemon wedges, with ½ tsp of salt, and cook over a low heat for five minutes. Serve immediately with lemon wedges.

Mejillones con azafrán y espinacas
Mussels with saffron and spinach

Serves 4–6 as part of a mixed tapas

150g (5½oz) spinach

olive oil

4 tbsp dry white wine

2 sweet white onions, finely chopped

4 bay leaves

1 celery stick, finely chopped (optional)

a few sprigs of thyme

10 black peppercorns

1kg (2lb 4oz) mussels, cleaned and debearded

1 tbsp unsalted butter

2 pinches of saffron strands

250g (9oz) crème fraîche

salt and freshly ground black pepper

In Spain there are many recipes for shellfish (or snails) with spinach or chard. Some are muddied with tomato purée, others flavoured with cloves. Often there is a handful of rice or some beans thrown in. (You'll find some of these recipes in the Rice chapter.)

This is a beautiful dish with golden creamy sauce and bright green spinach leaves contrasting wonderfully with the black and orange of the mussels.

✳ Wash the spinach, drain and then wilt it in a pan with a little olive oil. Don't overcook it. Set aside.

✳ Pour the wine into a large heavy-based pan with a tight-fitting lid. Add the onions, bay leaves, celery (if using), thyme and peppercorns and bring to a simmer.

✳ Now tip in the mussels and cover the pan, keeping it over a low heat. Shake the pan now and then to distribute the shellfish. Check to see that the mussels have opened and, when they are all open, tip the lot into a colander set over a bowl to catch the stock. Remove the flesh from some of the mussels and discard these shells. Discard any mussels that have refused to open.

✳ Wipe the pan and return it to the heat. Melt the butter and add the saffron, crème fraîche and the mussel liquor. Check for seasoning and add pepper. It's just possible you will also need salt, but mussel stock is usually salty enough. Bring to the boil and simmer for a couple of minutes, then return the spinach and the mussels. Cook for a minute to warm the mussels through, then serve immediately in warmed bowls with crusty bread.

Left: Mussels with saffron and spinach;
Far left: Moroccan peppered prawns

Algarvian 'fingernail' clams with coriander

Serves 4 as part of a mixed tapas

1kg (2lb 4oz) *conquilhas* or other clams

sea salt

3 garlic cloves, sliced

2 tbsp olive oil

handful of coriander leaves, finely chopped

freshly ground black pepper

splash of lemon juice, plus lemon slices to serve

This recipe is similar to Clams marinière (see page 98), but that Spanish recipe uses wine and parsley whereas this Portuguese recipe has lemon juice and coriander leaves. We tend to make this dish to serve as a tapa, as the tiny *conquilhas* are scarce and more expensive than clams; we make the Spanish version with regular clams for a main fish course or generous starter.

These little shellfish are unique to the waters of the Portuguese Algarve and the western shores of Andalusia; you could almost say they can only be found between the mouth of the Guadalquivir at Sanlúcar de Barrameda and west through to Sagres. The delicate shells hide sweet flesh and they are simple to prepare.

If you cannot get them (as well you may not!), use the same amount of regular clams, but buy the smallest you can find.

✳ Wash the clams and put them in salted water – as salty as the sea – to soak for 12 hours (or 'two tides', as they say in Portugal). If they are fresh, they will pump out any sand that may be inside them.

✳ Gild the garlic slices in the oil in a wide, heavy-based pan that has a tight-fitting lid. Reduce the heat and add the drained clams to the hot pan. Cover the pan and let the clams open over the heat, shaking from time to time. Check the clams after a minute to see if they have opened. If not, cook them for another minute or so. Take them off the flame as soon as they have all opened, or they will dry out. Discard any that have refused to open.

✳ Sprinkle with the coriander, grind on black pepper and add a squirt of lemon juice. Serve in little dishes with lemon slices.

Right: Algarvian 'fingernail' clams with coriander; Far right: Mussels with anchovies

Mejillones con anchoas
Mussels with anchovies

Serves 8–10 as part of a mixed tapas

3 large anchovy fillets (canned Anchoas del Cantábrico are best)

olive oil

leaves from 2 sprigs of parsley, finely chopped

leaves from 1 sprig of basil, finely chopped

2 garlic cloves, finely chopped

4 tbsp dry white wine

4 tbsp white wine vinegar

2kg (4lb 8oz) mussels, cleaned

150ml (5fl oz) double cream (optional)

freshly ground black pepper

If you tune into Seville's flamenco radio station, Radio Olé, you will regularly hear a *Sevillana* sung in honour of Galician mussels. The song is an advertisement in praise of the freshness of these mussels and acclaiming the high speed with which they are delivered to Andalusia from the Galician rias. This recipe is Catalan.

❀ Soak the anchovies in water for one hour, then drain and gently pat dry. Put them into a mortar and grind to a paste with the pestle.

❀ Take a wide, heavy-based pan that has a tight-fitting lid and add enough oil to cover the base. Place over a medium heat and sauté the herbs and garlic. Stir the ground anchovies, wine and vinegar together and add to the pan. Add the mussels and cream (if using), cover and steam until they open (a matter of three or four minutes, discard any shellfish that refuse to open). Toss, add pepper to taste and serve.

Anchoas en vinagre
Fresh pickled anchovies

Serves 8 as part of a mixed tapas

250g (9oz) fresh anchovies

sea salt

2–3 garlic cloves, finely sliced, plus more to serve

1 tbsp white wine vinegar

4–5 tbsp extra virgin olive oil, plus more to serve

leaves from 1 sprig of thyme

leaves from 3 large sprigs of flat-leaf parsley, finely chopped, plus more to serve

freshly ground black pepper

To eat these fresh we only buy small quantities, say 250g (9oz), enough to get on with for tapas one evening with other dishes.

❋ Rinse the anchovies under running water and place on a board. Cut off the heads. Insert the point of a knife into the anus of each fish and slice up to the head end. Wash out the guts. Open out each anchovy like a book, remove the spine and rib cage and discard. Salt them lightly and place in a shallow non-reactive dish.

❋ Mix the remaining ingredients except the pepper to form a marinade. Pour it over the anchovies and grind over black pepper. Cover and place in the fridge for a minimum of six hours.

❋ When you open the dish you'll find the fish has released liquid. Remove the fillets from the dish, discarding the liquid, place on a plate and sprinkle with garlic, extra virgin olive oil and parsley.

Bacalhau à brás
Salt cod with eggs and potatoes

Serves 4 as a hearty tapa or as a starter

400g (14 oz) dried salt cod
(preferably fillet)

500g (1lb 2oz) potatoes

sunflower oil, to deep-fry

3–4 tbsp olive oil

3 sweet white onions, very
finely sliced

1 garlic clove, finely chopped

6 free-range eggs

salt and freshly ground
black pepper

handful of black olives

handful of finely chopped
parsley leaves

Salt cod has been a staple in Spain and Portugal for hundreds of years. This is a Portuguese recipe which is also served locally in the Aracena mountains under the name of *Bacalao dorado*.

❋ Soak the salt cod (see page 101) for 24 hours, changing the water several times. Drain the fish, skin it and remove any bones you find. Shred the flesh with your fingers and place it into a dish.

❋ Cut the potatoes into very thin chips. Deep-fry the potatoes in very hot sunflower oil in a thermostat-controlled deep-fryer. You may have to do them in batches, to keep them crisp with the oil up to temperature. When they start to turn golden, lift the basket out of the fryer and drain the chips on kitchen paper.

❋ Both cod and chips can be kept to one side until you are ready to prepare the final dish.

❋ Now put a heavy-based casserole over a medium heat with the olive oil, onions and garlic and allow to cook gently until the onions are transparent. Add the shredded fish and stir thoroughly to coat in the oil. Add the cooked chips.

❋ Beat the eggs lightly and pour them over the whole. Taste and season with salt and pepper. Usually the fish will have retained some of its saltiness, so go carefully.

❋ Cook until the eggs have set creamily, then pour the whole into a serving dish, dot with black olives and sprinkle with parsley.

Cook's Note

Sunflower oil can reach high temperatures and should be used for hot frying. Olive oil should only be used for stewing, as it spoils at high temperatures and loses its health-giving properties.

Meat tapas

Huevos de codorniz con morcilla de Burgos
Quail's eggs on Burgos black pudding

These are one of my favourite tapas. Quail's eggs are a bit fiddly to
fry, only because cracking them is tricky as the membrane under
the shell is much tougher than that of a hen's egg. I use a sharp
knife and give a firm-but-gentle thwack, making a neat cut into
the shell. Sometimes you will need to unpick the membrane
with the knife point. Go carefully, so as not to cut into the yolk.

Serves 6 as part of a mixed tapas

olive oil

12 quail's eggs

12 thinnish slices of morcilla de Burgos

12 small regañá biscuits (made from unleavened bread dough), or mini rusks

freshly ground black pepper

12 thin slivers of jamón ibérico

Burgos black pudding is flavoured with onions and cumin. The starchy element is rice. It's not unlike the black puddings we used to get in Scotland, but there it would be made with oatmeal and flavoured with cloves, nutmeg and black pepper. Other good locally made black pudding of a diameter not bigger than the fried quail's egg itself will do. The sausage should be made with a proper animal gut casing, so avoid those large factory-made black puddings that come in a plastic 'skin'.

Put a little olive oil in a pan over a medium-high heat. Crack the eggs with a knife as described left, and open into the pan. Fry two or three at a time, but don't let them run together. I don't baste them as I like the bright yellow colour. They should be cooked, with soft yolks. Leave to drain on kitchen paper.

Fry the morcilla slices gently in the oily pan. They will release some fat. If they start to curl up, cut off the surrounding skin and press down on each disc. Turn and cook on the other side for a minute. It's fine if they are slightly crisp, but don't burn them.

Now, quickly place each slice of warm sausage on a biscuit or rusk, slide a quail's egg on top of each, sprinkle black pepper on the yolk, cover with a piece of jamón and, when you have done them all, serve immediately. It's important to eat these eggs while the black pudding is still warm.

Empanadas de carne
Meat pasties

We would use fresh Iberian pork, or possibly kid (young goat) for these meat pasties, but good-quality minced beef or pork would do just as well. We normally use empanada wrappers to make these, as do most people in Spain, but give the pastry recipe here for those who want it. Do feel free to use the wrappers instead, if you can find a shop that sells them, as it makes the process easier.

Serves 8 as part of a mixed tapas

For the filling

2 carrots, finely chopped

1 sweet white onion,
finely chopped

2 garlic cloves, finely chopped

250ml (9fl oz) olive oil, plus
more to cook the meat

250g (9oz) minced pork, or beef,
or a mixture

leaves from 2 sprigs of parsley,
finely chopped

8–10 mint leaves, finely chopped

1 tbsp tomato purée

salt and freshly ground
black pepper

For the pastry

250g (9oz) plain flour, plus more
to dust

1 tsp salt

75g (2¾oz) unsalted butter,
chopped into small pieces

2 free-range eggs, lightly beaten

✳ For the filling, fry the carrots, onion and garlic in a little olive oil until soft, then add the minced meat and most of the herbs, stirring the mixture and breaking it up with a spoon to brown all over. Cover and cook for about 45 minutes, then add the tomato purée and a little water if it is looking dry. When the liquid has been absorbed, add the remaining herbs, season and remove from the heat.

✳ At this stage you could cool the meat, then cover and place in the fridge until the following day. (If you do, allow the meat to return to room temperature before making the pasties.)

✳ To make the pastry, put the flour and the salt into a food processor fitted with the pastry blade. Whirr briefly to mix, then start to drop in the small pieces of butter until they have been incorporated. Don't beat until the butter gets hot, just do it quickly so that it looks like breadcrumbs.

✳ Tip in the eggs gradually, allowing them to be absorbed little by little until a ball of dough is formed. Remove with a spatula, wrap in cling film and chill it in the fridge for 30 minutes.

✳ Roll the pastry out on a lightly floured table until quite thin (2–4mm/⅛in thick). Cut into 6–7.5cm (2½–3in) discs with a cookie cutter or the top of a glass. Cover with a damp (not wet) cloth, so the discs don't dry out as you work.

✳ Take one disc at a time and moisten the rim with water. Place a spoonful of the meat on one half and fold over the other half, pressing together gently with a fork to seal. Make sure you don't get any oil from the filling on to the rim, or it won't stick down.

✳ When all the pastry or all the meat has been used up, put the 250ml (9fl oz) of olive oil in a deep pan over medium-high heat; the oil should come no more than one-third of the way up the sides of the pan. Fry the empanadas, turning them halfway through cooking, so both sides are golden brown.

✳ Drain the empanadas on kitchen paper, then place them on a pretty dish and serve. These are best eaten with the fingers, so have plenty of paper napkins to hand.

Paté de higaditos de pollo
Chicken liver pâté

Serves 16 as part of a mixed tapas spread on biscuits or tostadas, or 8 as a starter with salad and toast

225g (8oz) chicken livers, preferably organic

225g (8oz) unsalted butter, plus clarified butter made from 115g (4oz) unsalted butter, to seal (see below)

2 rashers of bacon (smoked if possible), chopped

1 large garlic clove, finely chopped

1 sweet white onion, finely chopped

2 tbsp Spanish brandy (Soberano, Veterano or 103)

leaves from 1 sprig of thyme

salt and freshly ground black pepper

fresh bay leaves, to serve

Delicious with freshly baked warm bread, or served on tostadas and topped with some caramelised onion.

❋ Wash the livers and remove any green-tinged bitter bits. Melt a little of the butter in a pan and gently fry the bacon, garlic and onion. When soft, add the livers and simmer gently. Do not overcook them or the outsides will get crusty, but make sure all traces of pink have gone. Add the rest of the unclarified butter, the brandy and thyme and cook for a short while to evaporate the alcohol. Season to taste and cool.

❋ Tip into a food processor and purée until smooth, then transfer to a dish or large ramekin and smooth the top. Seal by carefully pouring on the clarified butter.

❋ Decorate the top with a couple of fresh bay leaves when taking to the table and spread on tostadas or biscuits as a tapa, or serve with a side salad and thinly sliced toast for a starter.

How to clarify butter
Melt the butter in a pan until it foams. Skim off the foam. What is left is clarified butter. Carefully pour it from the pan; you want only the clear yellow liquid and not the milky whitish solids (throw the latter away).

Albóndigas con tomate
Meatballs in tomato and orange sauce

Serves 8 as part of a mixed tapas

4 spring onions, finely chopped

2 garlic cloves, finely chopped

225g (8oz) minced beef or pork or a mixture of chicken and pork

2 tbsp grated manchego cheese

2 tsp thyme leaves, plus more to serve (optional)

salt and freshly ground black pepper

1 tbsp olive oil, plus 2 tbsp more to thicken (optional)

4 tomatoes, chopped

200ml (7fl oz) red wine

2 tbsp chopped rosemary leaves

½ tsp caster sugar

a little finely grated orange zest, plus juice of 1 orange

2 tsp cornflour (optional)

chopped black olives (optional)

These tasty meatballs can be made with minced beef, or pork, or a mixture of chicken and pork. We like to use Iberian pork because it is readily available in the Sierra de Huelva and the quality can be relied upon. Have the butcher mince the meat in front of you.

❋ Mix the spring onions and garlic with the meat, cheese and thyme in a bowl and season with plenty of salt and pepper.

❋ Mould into little meat balls with the palm of your hand, then fry gently in the 1 tbsp of olive oil in a deepish pan, turning frequently until browned all over. Remove the meatballs, set on kitchen paper and keep them warm in a low oven.

❋ Add the tomatoes to the pan with the wine, rosemary, sugar and orange zest and juice and season with salt and pepper. Cook gently for 15 minutes or so.

❋ If the sauce is too thin, mix the cornflour with the 2 tbsp olive oil to make a paste. Whisk 1 tbsp of the paste into the sauce and bring it to the boil. Cook out until the sauce is thick and smooth (you probably won't need the rest of the paste, but keep it in case you want the sauce even thicker). Replace the meatballs and cook gently until warmed through.

❋ Serve sprinkled with chopped black olives, or more thyme.

Riñones al jerez
Kidneys in sherry

Serves 8 or more (there is always someone who does not eat offal) as part of a mixed tapas

500g (1lb 2oz) lamb's kidneys, preferably organic

salt and freshly ground black pepper

1 sweet white onion, finely chopped

6 tbsp olive oil

1 garlic clove, finely sliced

1 tbsp plain flour

½ tbsp smoked sweet paprika (pimientón dulce de la Vera)

leaves from 2 sprigs of parsley

leaves from 2 sprigs of thyme

125ml (4fl oz) fino sherry

Lamb's or pig's kidneys are perfect for this dish, and try to use a light fino sherry such as Tio Pepe or Fino Quinta.

✳ Put two or three fingers of water into a pan that has a lid and bring to the boil. Place the lid on the pan upside down.

✳ Trim the kidneys of their hard cores and peel off the membranes, then slice them. Put them in the upside-down lid, sprinkled with a little salt. Reduce the heat under the pan to low and allow the kidneys to sweat for 10 minutes, during which time they will have purged themselves of impurities. Now tip the kidneys into a colander or sieve and rinse under cold running water.

✳ Fry the onion in half the olive oil over a low heat in a big frying pan. When it is soft, add the kidneys and stir well. When they are sealed and coloured, add the garlic and the rest of the oil. Sprinkle with the flour and paprika and stir them in.

✳ Add 125ml (4fl oz) of water, the parsley and thyme and bring to a simmer. Season to taste and stir in the sherry just before serving.

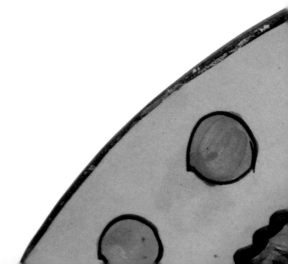

Ensalada de hígado de cerdo
Iberian pig's liver salad

Serves 8 or more (there is always someone who does not eat offal) as part of a mixed tapas

3 garlic cloves

olive oil

250g (9oz) Iberian pig's liver or lamb's liver, in one piece, preferably organic

125ml (4fl oz) Alfonso dry oloroso sherry

balsamic vinegar or sweet sherry vinegar

salt and freshly ground black pepper

leaves from 1 bunch of coriander, chopped

This delicious cold salad can be made with lamb's livers just as well. It's nearly always put on the table at the start of a meal in our local restaurants, and is happily accompanied by a glass of manzanilla.

❋ Slice two of the garlic cloves and fry them gently in a little olive oil, then add the liver. Fry until cooked through but still pink inside – four to six minutes depending on girth – then remove from the pan, put on a saucer and allow to cool.

❋ Deglaze the hot pan with the sherry, then pour it off into a bowl. Add some balsamic vinegar, salt and pepper and olive oil to the bowl and whisk with a fork to make a vinaigrette. Taste and adjust the levels of the ingredients until you are happy with the flavour.

❋ When the liver is cold, slice it into fingers on a wooden board. Put the liver fingers into a serving bowl, season with salt and pepper and toss in the vinaigrette.

❋ Finely slice the remaining garlic clove and add it to the liver with the coriander. Serve with crusty bread.

Jamón

We always have a jamón ibérico on a stand in the kitchen. It is a staple of the Sierra de Aracena, which is included in the denomination of origin of the renowned jamón de Jabugo. The village of Jabugo – internationally famous for its hams – is close to our farm, and we grow some pretty good hams, fattening our pigs on chestnuts, acorns from the cork oaks and pumpkins and pears from the orchards, as well as with any leftover vegetables and bread from our kitchen.

Jamón should be sliced very finely, almost paper-thin, with a very sharp, thin, long-bladed knife. It must never be served icy cold, but always at room temperature so the silky fat can melt easily on the tongue. It is traditional to serve jamón as tapas with little Andalusian bread sticks called *picos*.

Chacina

Chacina is the general word for our Iberian pork products, such as chorizo (cho-ree-tho, never cho-ritso!!), salchichón – which is akin to saucisson sec in France, or salami in Italy – and marinated air-dried fillets of Iberian pork.

We slice all these and serve them with *picos* bread sticks (see above), or we fry little round chorizo beads known as 'rosary sausages' and serve them with fresh bread.

Above: Jeannie carving our home-cured jamón; Right: one of our jamóns from a rear leg, identified by its 'V'-shape of peeled skin

Jamón

Finca Buenvino lies just 8km from the village of Jabugo, famous for its jamón, and our farm falls within the area of its denomination of origin. We make our own hams, and enjoy sharing them with our guests.

We do not have the ideal landscape of the *dehesa*, with its evergreen holm oaks that are so vital in the production of Iberian jamón de bellota (acorn-fed hams), but this has not discouraged us. For many years, we bred and raised our own pigs and made our own fruit- and chestnut-fed jamón, chorizo, salchichón and morcilla.

We discovered early on that breeding and rearing our own pigs was too complicated on our small, steep farm. The pigs had to survive through the summer months on a diet of fruit, vegetables and maize, and we had to keep them corralled in a one-hectare pen so we could get at them easily at feeding times. We also found that having guests and breeding pigs does not work together. The pigs, although over the hill behind our house, often brought wafts of unsavoury odours, and quantities of autumn flies!

We turned to buying in pigs at about one year old for making our own hams. We buy them in September or early October and set them free into the forest. The pigs snuffle around, eating roots and plants and the acorns of the cork oak, and fallen plums, pears and figs from the orchards. Later, when the chestnuts have been harvested, we move the pigs into the chestnut woods to forage for what is left on the ground. Our hams always taste great and we have the pleasure of knowing just what the animals have been eating.

The Iberian pig has the capacity to store fat inside its muscle tissue, which is not the case with a white pig. Think of a good old English pork chop: the actual meat is dry, while the fat lies around it. Good beef, on the other hand, has marbling thoughout the flesh, as is the case with Iberian pork. This preponderance of fat allows the meat to cure without drying out excessively and gives the unique, rich flavour.

After three or four months of blissful free-range 'pigging out', our pigs are ready to be killed. The climate is perfect; cold and frosty and – importantly – fly-free. After butchering the pigs, we chill the meat for 24 hours in the frosty air, then clean the legs thoroughly, peeling off the skin of the back legs, or hams, to show the fat in its characteristic 'V' shape. Front legs are peeled in a semi circle, so that hams and forelegs are instantly recognisable, even when cured.

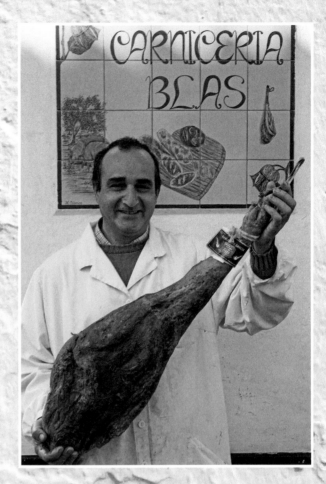

Our fresh hams then go into a large wooden box, on a bed of rock salt. They are packed side by side, hip to toe, then covered in another layer of rock salt. Finally on the top layer of salt we put the front legs, arranged in the same way. They always go near the surface because, being smaller, they require less time in the salt (just 10 days to a rear leg's 21 days). On the top of the last layer of salt the sign of the cross is made with the fingers and thumb, to ensure a good result. (Some people still pray to St Anthony Abbot, who is often portrayed with a pig at his feet and is perceived locally as the patron saint of farmers.)

Once the hams are extracted from the salt, they are washed down with warm water and a clean cloth, then hung in the drying room. Slowly, a beneficial mould grows on the surface of the hams (similar to the mould in a blue cheese) and every three weeks or so we wipe the surface of the hams with a cloth dipped in sunflower oil.

After a year, or 18 months, the shoulders (front legs) are ready for eating. The hams (rear legs) will take longer, around two years; sometimes longer for big hams.

The process in commercial ham-producing houses might be slightly different to ours, but in the essentials there is not much difference between small home production and high-end factory hams. In the Sierra de Aracena most families still kill their own pigs, although it is becoming more common for small farmers to send their pigs to the slaughterhouse. This is a shame, as a pig killing is a celebratory couple of days, when families have lots of spare food to offer to friends and relations as they work together making chorizo and salchichón, and marinading the loins in garlic and paprika to make *lomo embuchado*.

We look forward to attending our friends' *matanzas* as much as we enjoy hosting our own. Every pig-killing is an occasion for sharing gossip, exchanging recipes and advice, and binds us to the community in which we live.

Our good friend, Blas the butcher

Soup

There is a tradition of cold soups in Andalusia, notably the 'big three': gazpacho, salmorejo and ajo blanco. They are not only refreshing, but replace nutrients and body salts lost while labouring in the countryside in the blasting heat of summer.

Nowadays they have become part of the stock of traditional recipes in urban Spanish restaurants. New combinations appear now and then, not all of them entirely successful (watermelon gazpacho and strawberry gazpacho among them). The truth is that strawberries and watermelon become almost unidentifiable when salted and mixed with garlic and olive oil... it still takes a good, ripe tomato to produce the ideal gazpacho or salmorejo.

Gazpacho

Serves 8 as part of a mixed tapas

2 slices of stale white country bread, crusts removed

3 garlic cloves

salt and freshly ground black pepper, to taste

1 large green pepper, deseeded and chopped

½ cucumber, peeled

1kg (2lb 4oz) really ripe tomatoes, roughly chopped

5 tbsp extra virgin olive oil

1 tbsp sherry vinegar

400ml iced water

This refreshing soup is a cure all. It is even said that it can prevent hangovers. During the hot summers, it is traditional in some *sevillano* households to take a glass of this icy soup before retiring to bed at four or five in the morning after a long night of dancing and drinking! However it's equally delicious just before lunch, after a hot morning of working on the farm. This is a different concept to the restaurant type of gazpacho with its added garnishes; it is simple, honest and basic beyond belief, the ultimate pick-me-up.

Soak the bread in cold water, then wring it out. Put the bread, garlic and salt in a blender and process to a paste.

Add the green pepper and cucumber, then the tomatoes, and whizz until smooth. Slowly add the olive oil and sherry vinegar, then enough iced water to achieve the consistency desired; it should be easy to drink it out of a glass and you should have 400–500ml (14–18fl oz) of soup. Chill, then season to taste before serving in small glasses.

Salmorejo

Serves 8 as part of a mixed tapas, or 4 as a starter

4–6 slices of stale white country bread, crusts removed

1 garlic clove

salt and freshly ground black pepper

1 green pepper (or red for a more dramatic colour), deseeded and chopped

4–5 ripe red tomatoes, roughly chopped

125ml (4fl oz) extra virgin olive oil, plus more to serve

good wine vinegar (ideally sherry vinegar)

iced water, if needed

chopped hard-boiled free-range egg, to serve (optional)

chopped jamón (optional)

dried oregano (optional)

This is a typical thick soup from Córdoba, similar to gazpacho. It contains proportionately more oil and bread and so is richer, thicker and more creamy in texture. It can also be used (without the jamón and eggs sprinkled over) as a sauce for fish or meat.

❋ Soak the bread in cold water. In a mortar or food processor, grind the garlic, salt, green or red pepper and the tomatoes. Wring the water from the bread and add it, blitzing or grinding until you have a fine paste. Add the olive oil and mix until the paste is shiny.

❋ Now splash in a little vinegar to taste and mix it in well. Add a bit of iced water if the soup is too stiff; you should be able to pour it thickly from a jug on to a flat plate, then tilt the plate to distribute it evenly. Season to taste.

❋ Serve cold, topped with the hard-boiled egg and jamón (if using). Sprinkle with a swirl of extra virgin olive oil. At Finca Buenvino we always add dried oregano leaves from the forest.

Ajo blanco
Garlic and almond soup

Serves 8 as part of a mixed tapas, or 4 as a starter

For the soup

6 slices of stale white country bread, crusts removed

1 tsp sea salt, or to taste

2 garlic cloves, or to taste

2 good fistfuls of blanched almonds

100–120ml good-quality olive oil, to taste

2 tbsp white wine vinegar or sherry vinegar (the paler the better, for looks!), or to taste

iced water

To serve

120g seedless sultanas or raisins

150ml Pedro Ximenez sherry, or cream sherry

ground cumin, or toasted cumin seeds

extra virgin olive oil (optional)

This simplest of soups is the perfect example of how a picada is used to emulsify oil and water. Cold almond soup has always been made in the Montes de Málaga, the steep hillocks which cut off the coastal strip from the mountains and plains of Antequera. In late winter and early spring, the hills are covered in almond blossom. In isolated farmhouses this soup would have been a refreshing summer staple, for it is extremely nourishing. It would originally have been made in a mortar with a pestle, but nowadays it is easier to make it in a food processor.

You will also find ajo blanco on the menu in many top-class restaurants in Andalusia, where its simplicity and subtle blend of flavours is greatly appreciated. As it was a recipe handed down in families, there are many versions. Some use up to six cloves of garlic, some only use one. Use more garlic than called for here if you like, but in our opinion too much can overwhelm the subtle flavour of the almonds.

The sweetness in some recipes for ajo blanco is provided by peeled muscat grapes (also grown in Málaga for dulce wine). In Córdoba I have eaten the soup with slices of apple in the bottom of the dish, and I have heard of versions with melon, too.

At Finca Buenvino we usually serve the soup with raisins or sultanas soaked in sweet sherry and a dusting of ground cumin on top, as in the recipe given below. In another summer version, we grind plenty of basil and parsley leaves into the soup and make what we call 'ajo verde'.

❋ Soak the bread in water until soft, then wring it out. Place the salt, garlic and almonds in a food processor and grind finely.

❋ Grind the bread together with the almond mixture until you have a paste. Now, with the processor still turning, gradually pour in the oil.

❋ Immediately the oil has been absorbed, pour in the vinegar. Now add the iced water – little by little – until you have a thin, creamy texture.

✿Taste the soup, adding more salt or vinegar accordingly, and mix well. Pour into a bowl, cover and refrigerate.

✿While the soup is chilling, simmer the raisins with the sherry in a pan over low heat until all the sherry has been absorbed and the raisins have plumped up. Set aside to cool.

✿To serve, place a spoonful of raisins in the bottom of each bowl, ladle the chilled soup over the raisins, then sprinkle with ground cumin or toasted cumin seeds. Swirl on a little extra virgin olive oil, if you like, to serve.

Sopa de habas con papas
Broad bean and potato soup

Serves 8–10 as a starter

450g (1lb) large fresh (or frozen) shelled broad beans

2 tbsp olive oil

2 large sweet white onions, finely sliced

3 large floury potatoes, peeled and finely chopped

1.7l (3 pints) chicken stock

leaves from 1 bunch of coriander, chopped

150ml (5fl oz) single cream, plus more to serve (optional)

salt and freshly ground black pepper

extra virgin olive oil, to serve (optional)

In mid- to late-spring, when we have already had the best of the smallest broad beans, this is a good way to use those larger, floury ones. Spring weather in the Aracena mountains is hot in the daytime, but cool or even cold by night; so either method of serving this thick green soup – hot and comforting at night or cold and refreshing for lunch – is welcome at this time of year.

❋ Bring a large pot of water to the boil. Add the broad beans, return to the boil and cook for two or three minutes. Pour into a colander and rinse with cold water. Pinch and slip each bean out of its outer skin to reveal the bright green, tender bean within. Discard (or compost) the whitish, tough husks.

❋ Heat the 2 tbsp of olive oil in a large pan and fry the onions gently until soft (about five minutes).

❋ Add the potatoes, most of the beans (keep a few to one side) and the stock and bring to the boil. Reduce the heat to a simmer and cook for five minutes, then add most of the coriander (keep some to one side) and simmer for a further 10 minutes.

❋ Blend the soup in batches in a food processor or blender, then return to the rinsed-out pan.

❋ Stir in some of the cream, season, and return to the simmer if you're going to serve it hot. Alternatively, allow to cool, then chill in the refrigerator and serve cold. Either way, serve sprinkled with the reserved coriander and blanched, peeled green broad beans; the latter usually separate conveniently into halves which float happily on the thick soup.

❋ A swirl of cream or extra virgin olive oil completes the picture.

Arroz
Rice

Rice is grown just over an hour's drive away from our Finca, in the delta of the Guadalquivir south of Seville. It's a relatively new crop in the area, introduced in 1937 by the nationalist General Queipo de Llano, who saw it as a good way of feeding his troops after they had taken the south. The land was prepared with the assistance of 300 Valencian prisoners.

Andalusia produces one-third of all Spanish rice, though Valencia and Catalonia still offer the best examples of rice dishes, far subtler and more delicious than the often infamous tourist paella.

Rice can be dressed up or down, fit for a king, a businessman or a peasant farmer. It can be coloured with golden saffron, scarlet tomato or the smudgy grey of squid ink. It can be flavoured with mountain herbs and a humble rabbit or chicken, or with dark green chard dotted with the white shells of snails, or it can be gloriously rich with lobster and razor clams... though it is just as good with a strong tomato stock flavoured with onion and green pepper.

The peasant rice dishes, humble country affairs halfway between soup and risotto, are at their most delightful in autumn, when wild mushrooms are to be found in the woods. Here are a few other ideas to set you on your way.

Black rice, or 'dirty' rice (see overleaf),
with added peppers for colour

THE BUENVINO COOKBOOK

Black rice, or 'dirty' rice

Serves 12

1.5 litres (2½ pints) fish stock,
preferably home-made
(see page 83)

1 cuttlefish (250g/9oz), or
2–3 squid, cleaned and cut
into small pieces (see page 93,
or ask your fishmonger to do it)

olive oil

2 sweet white onions, chopped

2 large beef tomatoes, deseeded,
skinned and chopped (see page
96) or grated

550g (1lb 4oz) monkfish, or
any other firm white fish,
cut into 8 pieces

18 mussels, cleaned
and debearded

8 shell-on raw tiger prawns
(optional)

2 sachets of squid ink, or ink
sacs from the squid or cuttlefish

700g (1lb 9oz) paella rice

2 garlic cloves, finely chopped

leaves from 2 sprigs of parsley,
finely chopped, plus more
to serve

salt

We tasted our first black rice in the centre of Barcelona, cooked over a wood fire in the back yard of some old buildings not far from Las Ramblas. This is where our friends Toby and Xus had their living space and design studio in the late 1990s. To find it you had to walk through an arch off a narrow street into a courtyard, where artisan workshops and tall, charming old buildings were sadly scheduled for demolition. Our friends lived up an iron staircase in a glass-sided studio, with a sleeping platform above.

On a steamy summer's evening, after all the downstairs workshops closed and just as the sun was going down, candles were placed in glasses up the metal stairs to the studio and Toby lit a fire on the cobbles, using off-cuts from the carpenter's shop below. When the fire had subsided, an iron tripod was set up over it, with a wide paella pan on top. The smoke added charm to the dish and we drank a glass or two of good white Penedès wine as we watched the dark pan bubbling over the gentle flames and hot coals.

When you are buying the monkfish for this dish, ask the fishmonger for the head and bones (and ask him to remove and discard the gills). Use them to make the stock (see page 83).

The squid or cuttlefish ink is vital to the final flavour and colour of the dish. Your fishmonger will either set it aside for you, or you can buy frozen ink in sachets... in this case two sachets would do. If you have problems finding it, look online for stockists.

❋ Bring the fish stock to a boil in a pan, then reduce to a slow simmer. In a paella pan (or large earthenware dish) cook the cuttlefish or squid in a little olive oil until just done (two minutes).

❋ Add the onions, with more oil if needed, and cook until soft, then the tomatoes. Cook, stirring well, until they almost dissolve.

❋ Add the remaining fish and shellfish and mix in well. When the mussels have opened, take a few of the most handsome and keep them to one side to decorate the dish. Remove the others from their shells and discard the shells (also discard any mussels that refuse to open). Remove the prawns (if using) and put to one side with the mussels so they keep their bright colour.

❉ Add the ink to the cuttlefish pan. If you have ink sacs, place them in a sieve over the pan and crush them with the back of a spoon. Add the rice and stir until coated with the inky mixture. Slowly add the hot stock, stir and bring to the boil. Add the garlic and parsley and salt to taste.

❉ Reduce the heat and cook slowly for 15–20 minutes, until all the liquid is absorbed but the rice is still creamy. Don't stir.

❉ When the dish is ready, return all the shellfish, decorating with the pink prawns (if using) and the reserved mussels in their shells, orange side up. Remove from the heat, cover with a clean tea towel and allow it to stand for five to 10 minutes before serving. The rice will absorb the flavours as the tea towel absorbs the steam; heat will permeate the mussels and prawns on the top of the dish.

❉ Remove the tea towel when ready to eat and, before taking the pan to the table, sprinkle with parsley. Serve on warmed plates.

Arroz a la manera de la Sierra Norte
Rabbit rice from the Sierra Norte

Serves 4

1 or 2 rabbits, jointed by your butcher

salt and freshly ground black pepper

3 tbsp olive oil

2 sweet white onions, sliced

2 large red peppers, sliced

150g (5½oz) chorizo, skinned and finely chopped

2 large garlic cloves, finely chopped

60g (2oz) sun-dried tomatoes in oil, chopped (for home-made, see page 214)

280g (8fl oz) paella rice

300ml (10fl oz) good chicken or quail stock, preferably home-made, hot

juice of 1 lemon

175ml (6fl oz) fino sherry

1 tbsp tomato purée

2 bay leaves

2 cloves

1 heaped tsp ground cumin

juice of 1 orange, plus orange wedges to serve

60g (2oz) black olives

chopped parsley or coriander leaves, to serve

The Sierra Norte de Sevilla is a beautiful natural park halfway along the Sierra Morena which links the Portuguese frontier and Córdoba, cutting off the plains of the Guadalquivir basin from the flatlands of Extremadura. The area is famed for its olives, but there are also wild areas full of game: boar, red deer, partridge, hare and rabbit. The mysterious white-washed haciendas, with orange trees and towering date palms in their courtyards, date back to the 17th century and are surrounded by extensive olive groves and chestnut woods, which are coppiced for the sticks with which the olive trees are beaten at harvest time. Rabbits run wild under the olive plantations and are a popular dish in the area.

❋ Season the rabbit joints with salt and pepper. Heat 2 tbsp of the olive oil in a pan and, when it is fairly hot, add the rabbit, a few pieces at a time, and brown to a golden colour all over. Place them on a plate lined with kitchen paper and keep in a warm place. Repeat to brown all the rabbit.

❋ Add the rest of the olive oil to the pan and increase the heat. When it's hot, add the onions and peppers and brown them a little, stirring so they do not burn.

❋ Reduce the heat a little and add the chorizo, garlic and sun-dried tomatoes and cook until the garlic is turning a golden colour.

❋ Tip in the rice, stirring until coated with the oil, then pour on the hot stock, lemon juice, sherry and tomato purée and return the rabbit. There should be enough liquid for the rice to be entirely covered. If not, add a little water.

❋ Put in the bay leaves and cloves and bring to a simmer, cover with a lid, then reduce the heat and allow to cook gently for about 20 minutes. Don't stir the pot. Just before the rice is fully cooked, taste for seasoning and stir in the cumin. Pick out the rabbit and put it on top of the rice. Pour in the orange juice and cook it into the rice.

❋ Sprinkle with the olives and herbs and dot the wedges of orange around for colour contrast with the black olives. Allow to stand for a few minutes, covered with a tea towel, then serve on warmed plates.

Paella de mariscos
Shellfish paella

Serves 4

125ml (4fl oz) olive oil

12 medium-large shell-on raw tiger prawns

salt and freshly ground black pepper

8 mussels, cleaned and debearded

50ml (2fl oz) white wine

1 sweet white onion, finely chopped

1 garlic clove, finely chopped

½ red pepper, finely chopped

½ green pepper, finely chopped

120–150g (4–5½oz) peas, and 150g (5½oz) green beans if you like, cut into short lengths

1 bay leaf

200g (7oz) squid rings

2 tomatoes, deseeded, skinned and chopped (see page 96) or grated

400g (14oz) paella rice

12 clams, cleaned

1 litre (1¾ pints) hot fish and shellfish stock, preferably home-made (see Cook's note, right), plus more if needed

1 tsp smoked sweet paprika (pimientón dulce de la Vera)

good pinch of saffron strands

Paella has become a cliché, along with sangria, sombreros, flamenco and bull fights. It's a much-maligned dish and often served tired, badly cooked and filled with colourings in the tourist restaurants of the coast and the interior. I would not advise you to choose it when it has been sitting on display in the Plaza Mayor, or on the esplanade where touts call out to you to choose their restaurant. But yes, do go for it in a seaside *chiringuito* (summer beach shack restaurant) on the Costa del Sol, or the Costa de La Luz (respectively the Mediterranean and Atlantic coasts of Andalusia), where in summer it's prepared specially on a Sunday afternoon; or else try it in the cities of the rice provinces – Barcelona, Valencia or Tarragona – in a traditional specialist rice restaurant. When it is freshly and correctly cooked, there is nothing better.

I'm not personally crazy for the *mar y montaña* or surf 'n' turf version of the dish, preferring a good mountain version with rabbit or partridge, or a shellfish and fish version to celebrate the gifts of the sea. This recipe calls for shellfish and squid or octopus. It could be made more regal by adding a lobster, or langoustines (*cigalas* in Spanish).

❀ Put a paella pan on the heat with the olive oil and, when it is hot, add the prawns with a little salt. Cook them, turning, until pink all over, then remove them from the oil, set aside and keep warm. They will have left a little flavour in the oil.

❀ Next put in the mussels and the wine, with a meagre pinch of salt, and cover. As soon as the shells open and release their juices, set aside with the prawns. Discard any that refuse to open.

❀ Tip the onion and the garlic into the pan, followed a minute or two later by the peppers, peas, beans (if using) and bay leaf. Cook until they are soft, then add the squid rings and cook briefly. Pour in the tomatoes with their juice and taste the whole for seasoning.

❀ When some of the watery juice from the tomatoes has melded with the other liquids, add the rice and fry it up for a few minutes, stirring from time to time.

*If you have a friendly fishmonger,
you can get hold of fish heads and
bones to make the stock. Your bag of
bits should weigh about 500g. To these
should be added some monkfish or hake
pieces, some prawn shells and heads,
1 onion, 1 bay leaf and salt. Pour in
2 litres (3½ pints) of water. After
simmering it all together for a scant
30 minutes, liquidise it, bones and all,
then pass it through a fine sieve,
pressing out every bit of the precious
liquid with the back of a spoon.*

✴ Add the clams, hot stock and sweet paprika, stirring to incorporate the spices. Rub the pinch of saffron between index finger and thumb so that it breaks up over the pan.

✴ Now you must leave the rice to cook without touching it for about 20 minutes, until the stock has been completely absorbed. Remove from the flame, dot the mussels on the rice with the prawns, and cover the whole dish with a tea towel. Allow to stand for a few minutes so that the rice continues quietly to drink in the flavours. Serve on warmed plates, and enjoy it with an ice-cold glass of albariño wine.

Arroz caldoso con conejo y verduras
Soupy rice with rabbit and vegetables

Serves 4

150g (5½oz) dried butter beans

olive oil

salt and freshly ground
black pepper

1 rabbit (or chicken), roughly
1kg (2lb 4oz), jointed into small
pieces by your butcher

250g (9oz) green beans, chopped

1 sweet white onion, chopped

2 garlic cloves, finely chopped

2 artichoke hearts, finely sliced

1 roasted red pepper, skinned
and chopped (see page 134)

1 large tomato, deseeded
and grated

1 ñora pepper, soaked in warm
water, or 1 small chilli, deseeded

200g (7oz) podded and peeled
broad beans (see page 75)

400g (14oz) paella rice

pinch of saffron strands

Halfway between a risotto and a soup, this is a perfect easy midday dish, eaten in a soup bowl with a spoon. Spain has many *comidas de cuchara* (spoon foods) and they are never to be disdained. There is something comforting about them on a winter's day, or in the evening, which makes you feel you have truly come home, whether from a journey, or a day of problems in the office. The *comida de cuchara* can disconnect you from street life and bring you back into the intimate world of your family and friends.

This is a recipe for rice and rabbit but, if you are squeamish about rabbit, a good free-range chicken will do.

✴ The night before you make the dish, put the butter beans in a large bowl and cover plentifully with water. Soak overnight.

✴ Next day, drain the beans, put them into fresh water with no salt or flavourings and bring to the boil, then reduce the heat to a simmer and leave to cook while you prepare the other ingredients.

✴ Put a deep earthenware or cast-iron pot on to a medium-low flame and add olive oil and salt. Add the rabbit (or chicken) pieces and fry for about 10 minutes, turning from time to time, until they are golden all over.

cont...

✳ Add the green beans, onion, garlic, artichokes and roasted pepper. When these have begun to soften, add the tomato. Stir well and add the ñora or chilli pepper, along with 1.5 litres (2½ pints) of water.

✳ These preparations should have taken about 30 minutes. You are now ready to take the butter beans off the heat and drain them in a colander. Put them into the pot with the other ingredients and bring to the boil. Reduce the heat and simmer for about 45 minutes.

✳ At the end of this time, season and add the broad beans and rice. Rub the pinch of saffron between index finger and thumb so that it breaks up over the pan. Cook for about 20 minutes, without stirring. If the rice drinks up all the liquid and the dish looks too dry, add more water. Your rice should be a bit sloppy. Turn off the heat and let the rice stand, covered with a tea towel, for a few minutes.

✳ Serve in warmed wide soup bowls, with a spoon, knife and fork to attack all the goodness in front of you. A hearty red Cariñena wine would be the perfect accompaniment.

Grilling red peppers to roast them before skinning brings out their sweetness

THE BUENVINO COOKBOOK

Arroz con acelgas
Rice with snails and chard

Serves 4–6

100g (3½oz) dried pinto beans, or 250g (9oz) canned pinto beans (drained weight)

150g (5½oz) snails, cleaned and purged by the supplier

100ml (3½fl oz) olive oil

1 sweet white onion, finely chopped

2 very ripe tomatoes, deseeded and grated

250g (9oz) potatoes, finely chopped

2 large bunches of chard, cut into strips

175g (6oz) paella rice

a pinch of saffron strands

salt and freshly ground black pepper

We can buy snails in the market in Seville in springtime. We prefer *cabrillas* snails, whitish with a black spiral on their shells. If you are a vegetarian, then omit the snails, but if you are merely not mad for snails or cannot find these small fellows in the UK, you could substitute them with winkles. (Equally you could use clams, although here you are beginning to tamper seriously with the landlubberly flavour and character of the dish!) Like spinach, chard wilts down to nothing, so I do mean *large* bunches, the sort that fill your hands.

❋ If you are using dried beans, the night before you make the dish, put the beans in a large bowl and cover plentifully with water. Leave to soak overnight.

❋ Next day, clean the snails in various changes of water. Cover them with cold water, put them over gentle heat so that they emerge from their shells and, when they are all out, bring them to the boil. Drain and set aside.

❋ Drain the soaked dried beans, if using, and cover with fresh water, adding a good splash of the olive oil. Do not salt, or the beans will toughen! Bring to the boil, then reduce the heat and allow to cook slowly until they are done, 40–60 minutes.

❋ In another pan, heat the remaining olive oil over a medium-low heat and cook the onion, tomatoes and potatoes without colour. Add the chard. Allow to cook together for an hour, then stir in the rice, snails and drained beans.

❋ Rub the pinch of saffron between index finger and thumb so that it breaks up over the pan. Add 100ml (3½fl oz) of water, season with salt and pepper and cook for about 20 minutes, without stirring.

❋ Leave the rice to stand for five minutes or so, covered with a tea towel, then bring it to the table and serve it straight out of the dish, with thickly cut crusty bread. We would drink a chilled young purplish wine from Valencia or Alicante with this dish.

Pescado
Fish

The Spanish are perhaps the most avid consumers of fish and shellfish in western Europe and they are insistent on buying, selling, cooking and eating only the best quality obtainable. Even in the interior of the country it is always possible to obtain a wide variety of fresh fish, as well as fish and shellfish which have been immediately frozen after being landed out at sea.

We buy our fish from Luis Bustamante in Aracena. He has a large white van with a shark painted over the rear doors and, every Tuesday, he drives down to the fish markets of Isla Cristina or Huelva, where the trawlers come in from the Atlantic coast. He returns to the mountains with a new supply of spanking fresh fish and there is always a steady stream of appreciative housewives and restaurant owners in his shop the next day. Luis is the perfect fishmonger of imagination: always ready to laugh, pleased to advise on cooking ideas... and sporting a huge walrus moustache.

Sustainability and fish consumption are a delicate subject. Spain is the biggest consumer of fish in Europe, but it's also one of the biggest producers of farmed fish, thanks to the large amount of suitable coastline. In Galicia, mussels hang on rafts in deep tidal water, while the wide river mouths and protected lagoons of Cantabria form ideal

Our fishmonger Luis Bustamante holding a cazón, *a type of shark usually marinated in vinegar and spices* (adobo), *then battered and fried*

THE BUENVINO COOKBOOK

environments. In southern Spain clams are grown and trout, gilt head bream, sea bass and turbot are all farmed. These are the fish we are constantly offered in shops and markets.

Spain has been farming fish since the 1980s and the business has been on a roll. A start has been made on farming sole, red bream and octopus among other species. Spain takes all this very seriously. Fish is big business. The quality of farmed fish is excellent and there is a movement towards improving the welfare of farmed fish, thanks to the work of ecologists and animal welfare groups.

There is still much wild fish to be had, but new laws about net size, and a ban on throwing away accidentally caught small fish, will go some way to replenishing stocks.

When you shop for fish, do check the provenance, which is written on the labels where the fish is displayed. You can make a choice. To buy or not to buy. Ultimately it is up to the consumer whether he or she buys farmed fish or not.

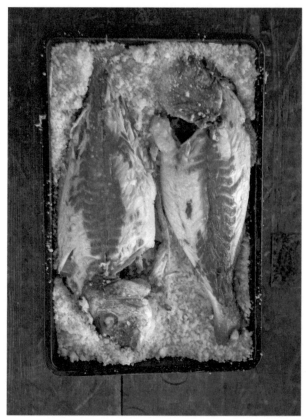

THE BUENVINO COOKBOOK

Dorada o lubina a la sal
Gilt-head bream, or sea bass, baked in salt

Serves 6–8

3–4kg (6lb 8oz–9lb) rough sea salt to cover a larger fish completely, or about 1kg (2lb 4oz) per smaller fish

1½–2kg (3lb 5oz–4lb 8oz) very fresh sea bream, or sea bass, or 6–8 x 350g (12oz) smaller fish, head on and guts in if possible

The chunky damp sea salt from the province of Cádiz or the salt pans of Valencia or Alicante forms the perfect crust, both protecting the fish from burning and sealing in the natural juices. You will need one large fish, or smaller individual fish. I think it's more of an adventure – and more spectacular – to use a big fish.

✳ Preheat the oven to about 240ºC/475ºF/gas mark 9, or as hot as it will go. Spread a layer of sea salt almost 2.5cm (1in) thick on an oven tray and lay the fish on top. Cover completely with the remaining salt. Pat it into place but, if it does not want to stay put, dip your fingers into a bowl of water and sprinkle some droplets on the salt, dry your hands and try again. The slightly dampened salt should be easier to shape.

✳ Place the salt-covered fish on the centre shelf of the oven, closing the door quickly so as not to lose any heat. Cook for 20–25 minutes for small fish and 30 minutes for a large fish.

✳ The fish will continue to cook in its red-hot crust, so do make sure everyone is at the table when you are ready to serve.

✳ Place the hot oven tray on to heatproof mats at the table and crack the crust open with a gentle but firm blow from the blunt edge of a knife or spatula. Insert the blade beneath the crust. Peel back the salt crust with the skin of the fish; try not to drop loose pieces of salt on the fish. The skin should come away easily, showing the lovely white flesh beneath.

✳ If serving a large fish, fillet it and serve a helping to each person.

✳ We like to serve this with a lemon hollandaise, or a mayonnaise gently flavoured with garlic, lemon and chopped parsley.

Cook's note

For cooking fish in salt, it is imperative that it be absolutely fresh. You are going to cook it with the head on and the guts in, so you don't want any hint of a tainted flavour. If you must gut the fish then get it done by the fishmonger and, when you get home, perhaps put some feathery fennel leaves in the cavity. Stuffed or not, make sure that the cavity is firmly sealed with cocktail sticks before cooking, otherwise the fish will take on too much salt.

Merluza con salsa verde
Hake with green sauce

Serves 4–6

2 tbsp olive oil

2 tbsp unsalted butter

1 sweet white onion,
finely chopped

2 garlic cloves, finely chopped

4 x 175g (6oz) hake fillets

salt and freshly ground pepper

2 tbsp plain flour

350ml (12fl oz) fish stock, ideally
home-made (see page 83)

175ml (6fl oz) dry white wine

250g (9oz) clams or cockles,
rinsed and purged (see page 54)

250g (9oz) mussels, cleaned
and debearded

200g (7oz) peas, cooked
(optional)

6 tbsp chopped parsley leaves

1 tbsp capers, drained and rinsed

Hake has been a staple for years all over Spain. Sam remembers it featuring on menus in the 1960s from the north to the south. It's a white flaky fish, easy to obtain filleted, so without the threat of bones which are so discouraging to the newbie fish eater.

When I ran one of my first cookery courses many years ago, we had a group of American ladies staying for the week and learning about food in Spain. On one of the last days of the week we drove down to Jerez to visit a winery. Afterwards, we headed for Sanlúcar de Barrameda, to eat fresh fish for lunch as we gazed out over the swollen yellow river across to the Coto Doñana nature reserve.

One of the ladies had told me she did not eat fish, and I warned her that she would be letting us down if she did not at least try something. Of course, I said, she could always have a steak, but that I would be disappointed if she did as this was a famous place for fish. 'What fish doesn't have a bone in it?' she enquired. 'You could try a swordfish steak,' I suggested.

Things were going swimmingly, piscatorially speaking, when I heard her cry out across the room 'Hey Betty! You could almost imagine you were eating a chicken nugget!'

I was not surprised to learn that she could not eat strawberries 'because of those little bitty eyes that look at you'. But mashed strawberries, thankfully, were 'just fine'.

❋ Heat the oil and butter in a large pan into which all the ingredients will comfortably fit, and fry the onion gently until soft, about five minutes. Add the garlic near the end of this time.

❋ Season the fish with salt and pepper and flour the pieces lightly.

❋ Push the onion and garlic to one side of the pan and add the fish, skin side up. Cook the fillets slowly, turning once, until golden.

❋ Add the stock and wine and bring to simmering point. Add the shellfish and, when the shells open, the peas (if using) and simmer for five minutes. Discard any shellfish that refuse to open. Stir in the parsley and capers and check the seasoning. Serve in soup plates.

Rosada con romesco

Ling with romesco sauce

Serves 6

6 ling fillets, or any firm white fish

plain flour

salt and freshly ground black pepper

olive oil

1 quantity Classic romesco or Our romesco (see pages 29 or 30)

Try any firm-fleshed white fish for this. We use ling fillets, but you could equally well use monkfish or hake. Romesco sauce is made with almonds, garlic, bread, peppers and tomatoes, all fried or roasted. You will find two recipes for it on pages 29 and 30.

Dip the fish briefly in a flat dish of flour, salt and pepper and fry quickly in olive oil, turning over when done on one side. When the fish is a light gold colour all over, it is ready. Put on a dish and keep warm until all the fillets are cooked.

Serve with romesco sauce.

Chipirones a la parrilla con ajo y perejil

Grilled squid with garlic and parsley

Serves 8–10

½ tsp salt

16–20 smallish (150g/5½oz) squid

200ml (7fl oz) extra virgin olive oil

½ sweet white onion, finely chopped

1 chilli, peeled, deseeded and finely chopped

4 garlic cloves, finely sliced

a little olive oil

2 tbsp finely chopped flat-leaf parsley leaves

To prepare squid, slide out the quill – which is like a piece of rigid cellophane – pull out the guts and peel off the mottled skin from the bodies and wings. Cut the tentacles from the heads. Discard the heads, guts, skin and quills. Rinse the tentacles and bodies, pat dry, then slice the bodies open, pulling our any remaining whitish innards. Score the bodies on the insides with a sharp knife. Messy, but strangely satisfying...

Salt the prepared squid and put in a shallow, non-reactive dish with all the other ingredients except the regular oil and the parsley. Cover and allow to marinate for 30 minutes to one hour.

Place a heavy cast-iron ridged grill over a gas flame, or on the barbecue, and allow it to heat. Grease it with a little oil. (If you prefer to cook on an open rack, and you have a good source of charcoal, then light the barbecue about 30 minutes before you plan to cook. When the coals are glowing, place the squid on the rack over the hot coals, about 20cm/8in above the source of heat.)

Left: Grilled squid with garlic and parsley

cont...

✳️ Grill the squid for five minutes on each side; no longer or it will become rubbery. You want some good black lines on the side of the squid if using the griddle pan, and some singeing of the tentacles if you are cooking over the open coals. The squid caramelises and becomes sweet where it is burned, which adds richness to a simple food. The art is to find the perfect balance between some caramelisation and keeping the meat tender.

✳️ To serve, toss some of the marinade into the pan for the last few seconds of cooking, then sprinkle with parsley. This is good with steamed potatoes and a green salad on the side.

Pulpo al horno con papas
Baked octopus and potatoes

Serves 6

1 thawed or pre-boiled octopus (see recipe introduction, right)

4 large tomatoes

150–200ml (5–7fl oz) olive oil

6 potatoes, cut into chunks

salt and freshly ground black pepper

3 garlic cloves, chopped

1 large sweet white or red onion, sliced

300ml (10fl oz) dry white wine

1 bay leaf

1 tbsp smoked sweet paprika (pimientón dulce de la Vera)

handful of parsley leaves, finely chopped

Many years ago, we were taken to a small shack in the marshes on the shore of the Ria Formosa in the Algarve, just two hours by car from our home. Inside-out octopuses were draped on fences like so much laundry hanging out to dry and, inside the ramshackle building, fishermen sat at oilcloth-covered tables. An elderly woman and her assistants roasted tray after dented aluminum tray of octopus, potato and tomato cooked in olive oil and paprika. When we got home, we just had to try to recreate this simple but delicious dish.

We use pre-boiled octopus which we can purchase from any supermarket or fishmonger in Spain. In the UK it's more common to get them frozen raw. If yours is frozen, allow it to thaw in a bowl in the fridge without removing the packaging. If you have raw octopus you will need to cook it first in boiling salted water for 30 minutes, then treat it as below.

✳️ Slice the octopus tentacles into pieces about 2.5cm (1in) in length. Slice open the body, then, after discarding the hard beak, the eye and the gunge inside the head, slice it into strips.

✳️ Preheat the oven to 180ºC/350ºF/gas mark 4.

cont …

✳ Boil a kettle and pour the hot water over the tomatoes in a bowl. When they are cool enough to handle, slip the skins off the tomatoes and quarter them.

✳ Tip the oil into an oven tray, wide and deep enough to hold all the ingredients, and place it over a medium heat. Add the potatoes, salted and peppered, and fry gently for a minute, but do not burn! Now add the garlic and onion and fry until wilted, stirring now and then. Don't break up the potatoes. Now add the tomatoes, wine, bay, paprika and 300ml (½ pint) of water.

✳ As soon as everything is warm, cover the oven tray with foil and slip it into the oven. 'Ah, but you have forgotten the octopus!' you will cry. No... it's just that there is nothing sadder than overcooked octopus. You only want it to heat through, and take in the mingled flavours from the sauce.

✳ Bake for 15 minutes, remove from the oven, add the octopus pieces and bring the dish to a gentle simmer. Cover with foil once more and return to the oven for 15–20 more minutes. The potatoes should be soft and the octopus not overcooked. If the dish looks dry, stir in a little more water towards the end of cooking.

✳ To serve, remove the dish from the oven, sprinkle with parsley and ladle into wide soup bowls. Bread, as usual, is a great idea, or just mash your potatoes into the juices.

Zarzuela de pescado
Stew of mixed fish

Zarzuela means an assembly or mixture. It is also the word for the Spanish operetta. This dish is made from a mixture of white fish and shellfish. The marine ingredients suggested below are only a guideline and can be varied at will so, if you are reading this on the shores of the Pacific, feel free to use snapper!

Sometimes we serve this with a spoonful of crème fraîche on each plate. If you prefer a thicker sauce, crush some of the croutons in a mortar with the chives and add them to some of the cooking liquid, then stir the mixture back into the dish five minutes before the end of cooking.

Serves 6

150ml (5fl oz) olive oil, plus more for the croutons

12 raw king prawns, shell on (cooked may be used if raw are unavailable)

1 large sweet white onion, finely chopped

3 garlic cloves, finely chopped

2 large tomatoes, grated, skins thrown away

2 tbsp chopped parsley leaves

salt and freshly ground black pepper

2 tbsp Spanish brandy

1 bay leaf

1 tsp smoked sweet paprika (pimientón dulce de la Vera)

½ tsp smoked hot paprika (pimientón picante de la Vera)

250ml (9fl oz) fino sherry or dry white wine

150ml (5fl oz) fish stock, preferably home-made (see page 83)

pinch of saffron strands

6 fish steaks (hake, monkfish, cod, halibut, turbot)

6 small squid, cleaned (see page 93), bodies cut into rings

12 mussels or clams

2–3 slices of stale white country bread, crusts removed, cut into cubes

chopped chives, to serve

Above right: Stew of mixed fish;
Left: a version of zarzuela *without tomato*

✳ Heat the oil in a very large frying pan that has a lid and, if using raw prawns, sauté until pink. Remove from the pan. *Do not overcook.* Set aside.

✳ In the same pan, fry the onion and garlic together for a minute or so but do not burn, then add the tomatoes, parsley and salt and pepper. When the onion has softened, pour on the brandy and ignite it. When the flames have subsided, add the bay leaf, paprikas, sherry or wine and stock and rub the saffron into the pan between your fingers and thumb. Stir together well.

✳ Put in the fish steaks and squid, bring to the boil, then reduce the heat to a simmer and cook for about eight minutes. Put in the mussels or clams, cover and cook until they open (discard any that refuse to open). Replace the prawns and cook for a couple of minutes to warm them through. Discard the bay leaf.

✳ Meanwhile, to make the croutons, fry the bread in olive oil until golden. Transfer the *zarzuela* to a warmed serving dish and strew with croutons and chives.

Prawns in garlic and chilli oil

This is an Andalusian classic, served in almost every bar and restaurant. It is perfect as a tapa, served with a selection of other dishes, or else it can be the starter to a more structured meal. Fresh crusty bread is essential for dipping into the spicy oil.

Peeled medium-sized prawns, tiger prawns or king prawns are all equally good here. You can leave the tails on, if you like.

Serves 8 as a starter or
12 as part of a mixed tapas

5 tbsp good olive oil

3 garlic cloves, finely chopped

2 dried chilli peppers (*guindillas*)

pinch of smoked hot paprika (pimientón picante de la Vera)

1kg (2lb 4oz) raw prawns (see recipe introduction)

sea salt

✷ Put the olive oil, garlic, chillies and paprika in a flameproof earthenware dish. Place over a medium heat until the oil begins to sizzle. Meanwhile, shell, devein if necessary and wash the prawns. Dry them with kitchen paper and add to the dish.

✷ Cook the prawns for about six minutes, turning halfway through if the oil is not deep enough to cook both sides. They are cooked when they turn pink and curl slightly.

✷ Sprinkle with salt and serve immediately, with chunks of crusty country bread. This dish is usually taken to the table red hot, with the oil bubbling, so do warn your table fellows to be patient and to take care not to burn themselves.

Clams marinière

Serves 4–6

500g (1lb 2oz) small clams

4 garlic cloves, chopped

handful of finely chopped parsley leaves

freshly ground black pepper

leaves from a sprig of thyme

150ml (5fl oz) dry white wine (see Cook's note, overleaf)

4 tbsp extra virgin olive oil

If the weather has been rough on the Costa de la Luz or in the Algarve, our clams can arrive a little gritty from the fish markets. Just to make certain, we always purge them before cooking. I would suggest that you do the same. When you are planning to have these clams for supper, purchase them in the morning and put them in a shallow tray or dish of salted water to purge for the day, to get rid of any traces of sand. If the clams are fresh, the salt will have them pumping vigorously. Don't make the water too salty, but try to match the saltiness of the sea itself. (Taste the salty water before you put the clams into it.) Change the water twice during the day, to get rid of grit.

cont...

For this recipe, try a wine from the Condado de Huelva or from Cádiz, such as El Castillo de San Diego, made by Barbadillo in Sanlúcar de Barrameda, Cádiz Province.

🌸 Place all the ingredients, including the clams, in a large pot that has a lid. Turn the heat to high. Bring the liquid to the boil, then reduce the heat to a simmer and cover the pot. The clams will steam gently and open; shake the pot occasionally. After five minutes, check the clams and, if they are all open, they're ready. If they're not, cover them again and let them cook for two or three minutes more. If any refuse to open, discard them.

🌸 Serve with plenty of bread for those who like to dip, otherwise eat the broth with a spoon.

Bacalao pilpil
Salt cod with chilli and garlic

Serves 4

450g (1lb) salt cod fillet

150–300ml (5fl oz–½ pint) extra virgin olive oil, depending how much sauce you want

4 garlic cloves, finely chopped

½–1 small dried chilli, soaked, or 2 fresh chillies, deseeded

leaves from 2 sprigs of parsley, finely chopped

freshly ground black pepper

Salt cod has been a staple of the Basque country for many centuries. Basque fishermen were some of the earliest Europeans to know where the shoals lay in the north west Atlantic. Extra virgin olive oil, in which the fish is cooked in this recipe, melds with the gelatine from the skin of the fish to form a thick mayonnaise-like sauce. To achieve this, the pan must be constantly moved and the temperature kept low. The technique is not at all difficult, but it does need your attention. It is said that fishermen discovered this method by accident when cooking the cod at sea during a rough storm, which tossed the fish about in the pan. You will need a small steel-meshed sieve or strainer.

🌸 If you have one large piece of salt cod, cut it into three or four smaller pieces. Put the fish in a large bowl and cover with cold water. Leave to soak for 48 hours, ideally under a dripping tap or, if not, change the water four times.

🌸 Drain the cod, give it a good rinse in fresh water, then pat dry with kitchen paper. Be careful to remove all the water by pressing down on the fillets gently with the paper. Remove any dangerous-looking bones with a pair of tweezers, but do not remove the skin as this contains the magic ingredient which will meld with the olive oil to make the sauce.

cont...

❉ Heat the oil in a wide, fairly high-sided pan. The best is either terrcotta or cast iron. You will need constant gentle heat when cooking the fish, and constant movement, but you do not want the oil to splash out over the edge.

❉ Sauté the garlic and chilli for two or three minutes until golden. Scatter in the parsley, stirring for about a minute, then remove everything from the oil with a slotted spoon and set aside.

❉ Reduce the heat to very low. Add the fish to the pan, skin-side down, and poach. Do not fry at high heat or you will ruin the oil and brown the skins, and it will not be possible to make the sauce which is the most distinctive part of this recipe. Move the pan in a circular motion almost constantly while the fish is cooking, or slide the fish about gently from time to time with a wooden spoon. It's important to keep up this movement while the fish is cooking, so the gelatine in the skin is released into the oil and begins to make a thin custard. Some whitish bubbles in the oil are a sign that the gelatine is beginning to be released from the skins. The oil will start to froth around these white spots.

❉ When you see the flesh of the fish begin to separate into ridges, it has been cooked sufficiently. Remove it with a slotted spoon and keep it warm in a low oven in a preheated serving dish.

❉ Now get working on making an emulsion of the oil. It should be warm rather than hot. Take a small metal sieve and lower it into the warm oil until it is resting on the bottom of the pan. Now shake it about gently over a low heat, where you see the bubbles of gelatine forming. Work it around in a circular or sideways motion and you will see the oil begin to thicken. If this does not happen immediately, dip your fingers into a bowl of cold water and splash some droplets of water into the oil. Start once more, concentrating on one area at a time, then gradually moving from one part of the pan to the other until the whole lot of oil has thickened into a mayonnaise-like sauce. When the sauce is done, pour it over the fish and grind on some black pepper.

❉ Decorate with the fried garlic, chilli and parsley and bring to the table. Simple steamed potatoes are the way to go.

Potatoes in almond sauce with salt cod

Serves 4

250g (9oz) salt cod fillet, soaked
(see page 101)

120ml (4fl oz) extra virgin
olive oil

thin slice of white country
bread, crusts removed

3 tbsp finely chopped garlic

10 blanched almonds

2 tbsp chopped flat-leaf
parsley leaves

1½ tsp turmeric

salt and freshly ground
black pepper

2 tbsp white wine vinegar

6 potatoes, peeled and cut
into cubes

This delicious dish used to be served locally in the more remote and old-fashioned establishments; small village hotels where travelling salesmen stopped over for a hasty lunch, or spent the night before moving on to Portugal on then slow and difficult roads. I've not come across it over the last few years, and wonder if it has fallen from favour as a restaurant dish because it seems too rustic. If so, it's a real shame. Try it.

❉ Soak the cod as on page 101, then remove the skin and any bones you come across and shred the flesh with two forks, or by hand.

❉ Heat the oil in a pan. Fry the bread, garlic and almonds in turn until golden, but do not allow to brown or they will spoil the flavour and colour of the dish. Remove from the oil with a slotted spoon.

❉ Add the parsley and toss in the hot oil for a moment. Remove when crisp. Reserve the oil.

❉ Make a picada: pound the fried parsley, bread, almonds and garlic in a mortar to form a paste. Add the turmeric, salt and pepper and continue pounding until well blended. Add a little water if the mixture is too thick. Add half the vinegar.

❉ Place the potatoes in a pan and cover with cold water. Pour the paste mixture over the potatoes and add the reserved oil. Stir well.

❉ Cook, uncovered, over a medium-low heat until the potatoes are tender, adding the flaked fish about five minutes before the end of cooking. Season with pepper. Taste for seasoning, adding more salt and the remaining vinegar if required.

❉ Serve with green beans or with sliced cooked beetroot tossed in butter and lemon juice.

Aves
Poultry

The first time we bought chickens to supply us with eggs, the poultry merchant's wife, Pepa, handed us three pieces of twine cut to the same length and showed us to a dark cobbled ramp (half staircase) that led to a basement stable off the back yard. 'Catch whichever you fancy!' she called after us.

There was a terrible clucking and fluttering and clouds of dust rose in the dark cellar, illuminated by narrow sun beams which came through a small window. After much squawking we did as we were told, tying the indignant hens together in pairs, the left foot of one tied to the right foot of the other, and we carried three pairs of hens upstairs by their feet, in which position they immediately seemed to become entranced.

The children were excited when we drove back from Aracena with the six young pullets scrabbling around in a large cardboard box. After the 10-minute drive we watched happily as they were released into their woodland pen that we had carefully fenced against mongoose, fox and genet cats.

For the recipes that follow, use free-range poultry.

Our cockerel and some of his girls

Codornices con membrillo
Quails and quince

Serves 8

225g (8oz) quince cheese, shop-bought or home-made (see page 210), or 4 quinces (if in season)

lemon juice (if using fresh quinces)

16 quails

salt and freshly ground black pepper

8 rashers of streaky bacon

150ml (5fl oz) white wine

In spring, the meadows at the bottom of our valley are filled with bird song and the pale pink blossom of the quince trees, which seem to bloom in every hedgerow and stream bank. The blossom is set off well by the pale apple-green leaves. In Spain an Indian summer is known as *el verano de membrillo* (a 'quince summer'). The phrase brings to mind those bright, clear-skied days when the russets, yellows and reds of the autumn foliage jump out against the blue sky and the quince and pear trees are loaded with scented fruit.

It is thought that Moorish conquerors brought the quince to the Iberian peninsula, and indeed there is nothing more exotic than the sweet, scented flavour of cooked quince. If fresh quinces are not in season, use quince cheese instead. In Britain, you can buy this from good cheese shops or the cheese section of larger supermarkets, or make your own (see page 210).

❋ Preheat the oven to 170ºC/340ºF/gas mark 3½. Use an ovenproof dish that will fit the quails snugly.

❋ If using quince cheese, slice it evenly over the dish. If using fresh quinces, core and thickly slice the fruit and drop the slices into water acidulated with the lemon juice to stop them turning brown.

❋ Pack the quails into the chosen dish and season them well. If using fresh quinces, slip a slice of quince between each bird. Put ½ a rasher of bacon on top of each quail and pour on the wine.

❋ Roast in the hot oven for 30 minutes. Serve with Potatoes baked in chicken stock (see overleaf) and perhaps a spinach purée.

Papas panaderas
Potatoes baked in chicken stock

Serves 8

1.5kg (3lb 5oz) potatoes

salt and freshly ground
black pepper

1 large sweet white or red onion,
finely sliced

50g (1¼ oz) unsalted butter, plus
more for the top

olive oil, for the dish

3 bay leaves

about 1 litre (1¼ pints) chicken
stock, preferably home-made

If you are cooking these potatoes to serve with Quails and quince (see previous page), put them on the top shelf of the preheated oven about 15 minutes before the quails, with the temperature increased to 180ºC/350ºF/gas mark 4. Then move them down to a lower shelf when the birds go in and the oven temperature is reduced for them. When the quails are done, keep them warm. Check the potatoes with a skewer to see if they are cooked through. If not, give them five minutes more while the birds rest.

❋ Preheat the oven to 180ºC/350ºF/gas mark 4. Peel and slice the potatoes finely and season with salt and pepper.

❋ Place the onion in a pan with the butter and soften over a gentle heat without burning, stirring from time to time.

❋ Arrange a layer of potatoes in a well-oiled ovenproof dish, then add a layer of onions, followed by another layer of potatoes. Continue alternating layers until everything has been used up, but finish with a layer of potatoes, arranged neatly.

❋ Put the dish on to an oven tray, as there may be some over-spill while the potatoes are cooking. Dot the top with some butter and fit the bay leaves down the sides of the dish. Heat the stock in a pan and pour it over the potatoes until the liquid reaches to the top. Cover with greaseproof paper and, if you have some weights, place them on top of the dish to keep the spuds well pressed down for a denser potato 'cake'.

❋ Bake the potatoes in the hot oven for 45 minutes. For a simple hearty meal with close family or friends, serve straight from the dish. If you prefer a more elegant presentation, cut out rings of the potato with a pastry or biscuit cutter. With the quails on the previous page, this is a perfect autumn dish with which to enjoy a glass of Ribera del Duero crianza.

Pollo en pepitoria
Chicken pepitoria

Serves 6–8

2 handfuls of blanched almonds

3 tbsp olive oil, plus more
if needed

5 garlic cloves, finely chopped

1 thick slice of stale white
country bread, crusts removed

2 x 1–1.5kg (2lb 4oz–3lb 5oz)
chickens, jointed

salt and freshly ground
black pepper

pinch of saffron strands

pinch of freshly grated nutmeg

2 cloves

½ tsp cumin seeds

450ml (¾ pint) good chicken
stock, preferably home-made

225ml (8fl oz) fino sherry

2 bay leaves

2 sprigs of thyme

handful of finely chopped
parsley leaves

squeeze of lemon juice

This and the next recipe are typical of Spanish chicken cookery;
the bare bones of how the bird is treated at the outset are identical.

This is also the perfect dish to demonstrate how to use a picada
(see pages 22–33). Look out and see what happens to the almonds,
bread and garlic in the last few minutes of cooking.

❋ Fry the almonds in a casserole with a little of the olive oil until
golden brown. Remove with a slotted spoon. Add the garlic cloves
with the rest of the oil and fry, but don't allow them to burn.
Remove with a slotted spoon. Fry the bread quickly and reserve it
with the garlic and almonds. This is the basis of your picada.

❋ Season the chicken pieces with salt and pepper and fry them in
the casserole until golden brown, about 10 minutes. If there isn't
enough oil add more, but the chicken should render its own fat.
Remove the chicken and drain off any excess fat from the pan.

❋ Now, grind the saffron in a mortar with the nutmeg, cloves and
cumin. Toss the spices around the hot pan until slightly toasted and
immediately add some of the stock to stop them burning. Wash out
the mortar with the sherry and tip it into the pan with the rest of
the stock. Stir to deglaze the pan. Return the chicken, add the bay
leaves and thyme and cover. Cook for 20 minutes.

❋ For the picada, grind the fried almonds, bread and garlic in a
mortar or a food processor and stir them into the sauce with the
parsley and lemon juice. The sauce will thicken.

❋ Serve with rice or couscous, and Spinach with raisins and pine
nuts (made in the same way as Spinach and chickpeas, see page 48,
only using pine nuts and raisins instead of chickpeas).

Pollo al ajillo
Garlic chicken

Serves 6–8

2 heads of garlic

3 tbsp olive oil, plus more for the chicken

2 x 1–1.5kg (2lb 4oz–3lb 5oz) chickens, jointed

salt and freshly ground black pepper, plus a small handful of black peppercorns

2 bay leaves

200ml (7fl oz) fino sherry

As in the previous recipe, your Spanish butcher will have ruthlessly hacked your chicken into smallish chunks, cracking through bones to release the stock. Your English butcher will have jointed the bird correctly, in a more restrained manner. Don't worry; either way works and you are less likely to catch yourself on a splinter of bone if the second method was used!

This recipe will have garlic fearers and vampires running for their lives, but don't worry; the enormous quantity of garlic used is the whole point. Remember that whole cloves treated this way will reduce to a sweet, caramelised texture without the fearsome burn of chopped raw garlic. The chicken juices, the fino sherry and the bay leaves, pepper and garlic form a rich, moreish sauce.

❋ Divide the heads of garlic into cloves, removing the loose bits of outer skin but leaving on the inner layer. Crack the garlic cloves slightly with the flat of a knife and place them in an earthenware or enamelled cast-iron casserole with the 3 tbsp of olive oil.

❋ Season the chicken pieces with salt and pepper and fry them in a large frying pan with a little more olive oil, turning them until golden brown, about 20 minutes. If there isn't enough oil add more, but the chicken should render its own fat.

❋ Remove the chicken and place on top of the garlic cloves with the bay leaves, sherry, 200ml (7fl oz) of water and some salt and peppercorns. Cover the casserole and place on a low heat. The chicken will now steam through as the garlic cooks.

❋ After 10 minutes or so, remove the lid and reduce the liquid. The chicken and garlic should be sticky in the bottom of the pan.

❋ Serve with a green salad and possibly some mashed potato to mop up the fragrant juices.

Pollo con ajonjolí para romerías
Romería chicken

Serves 6

4 tbsp turmeric

6 tbsp plain flour

salt and freshly ground black pepper

white sesame seeds

6 chicken breasts, thinly sliced

olive oil

finely chopped parsley or coriander leaves, to serve

This is an excellent lunch, served either hot or cold. We often serve a romesco sauce with it (see pages 29 and 30). It is a most useful summer dish for a lunch party to eat with a selection of salads, pastas and tortillas, salchichón and jamón as well as houmous, tahini and chicken liver pâté. Our favourite use of it is as a picnic food, it's easy to prepare and transports wonderfully; perfect for a romería, for which we name it.

A romería is a local pilgrimage and there is usually one or another taking place in one of the villages in the Sierra from May to September. Each romería varies in character: in Los Marines, Our Lady of Grace, patron of the village, is carried out of the church on the shoulders of the men, some bare headed, some wearing a sombrero, still other in flat caps. She rides on a gilded float with cushions of flowers beneath her feet. Horses jostle and the band plays the national anthem as she comes out of the church. There is a communal cry of *"¡Viva la Señora de Gracia!, ¡Viva la Virgen de los Marines!"* and, after the three cheers, she is carried out into the streets of her town. The band plays some solemn marches and the Ave Maria. Bells are rung enthusiastically by small boys perched in the top of the bell tower, rockets are fired into the blue sky to explode with a sharp crack and a puff of smoke... and the crowd moves forward.

The romería is one of the days which marks the cycle of the year, it's as if the hand were pointing at twenty past the hour. Held on the last Sunday of May, we know gardens have been sown, potatoes are in the ground and that our tiny pepper plants, aubergines and tomatoes will survive because the frosts are over for the year. Olives are ripening on the trees. The meadows are full of flowers: purple, yellow, white and scarlet. There is still rain to come before the heat.

Tables are laid out under the trees, great plates of jamón, chorizo and salchichón appear, along with picadillo, tortillas, cold garlic chicken, tomato salads and breaded pork chops.

It's a great day out for everyone. It keeps everybody up to date with family news and village gossip. It consolidates a community. It's often dark by the time the national anthem is played, the bells are rung and thanks are given for Her safe return to Her niche in the reredos, whence Her benevolence beams out for the rest of the year.

cont...

❋ Mix the turmeric and flour on a plate and season with salt and pepper. Sprinkle sesame seeds on another plate. Dip the chicken slices into the flour mixture, then into the sesame seeds, pressing down so that the seeds stick to the meat.

❋ Fry two or three slices of chicken at a time in olive oil, turning once, until golden. Drain on kitchen paper. Be careful not to get the bright yellow oil on to your clothes.

❋ Place on a large flat serving dish, sprinkle with parsley and eat hot, otherwise leave to cool. In Spain, many foods are eaten tepid.

Pollo con limón y jengibre
Lemon and ginger chicken

Serves 10

150ml (5fl oz) olive oil

2 x 1–1.5kg (2lb 4oz–3lb 5oz) chickens, jointed

1 sweet white onion, finely chopped

piece of root ginger about the size of a small egg, finely chopped

finely grated zest and juice of 2 unwaxed lemons

600ml (1 pint) double cream, or to taste

salt and freshly ground black pepper

2 tbsp chopped coriander leaves

Although I've not used cream in many of my recipes, I have snuck it in here as it is so delicious for the final sauce, much as in my Rabbit with cream and mustard (see page 120). Perhaps I am harking back to my classical training, but frankly it's a bore being a goody goody and a purist and always sticking just to olive oil, garlic and bay leaves. Let's ring the changes.

❋ Put the olive oil into a wide non-stick pan and brown the chicken pieces slightly over a moderate heat, starting skin side down, then turning halfway. When golden, toss in the onion and reduce the heat to allow the onion to wilt.

❋ Now add the ginger, lemon zest and juice, pour in the cream and season as you see fit. Cover the pan, reduce the heat to low and allow to cook slowly for 30 minutes.

❋ Remove the chicken from the pan and keep it warm in a serving dish. Bring the sauce to the boil for about one minute, then pour it over the chicken, sprinkle with the coriander and serve.

Magret de pato con oloroso dulce y naranjas
Duck breasts with orange and sweet oloroso sherry

Serves 8

3 duck breasts, about 350g (12oz) each

sea salt and freshly ground black pepper

honey

juice and finely grated zest of 2 oranges

150ml of sweet oloroso sherry, such as Gonzalez Byass Solera 1847

1 tsp cornflour (optional)

Duck breasts feature commonly nowadays on Spanish menus all over the country, though originally they were a speciality of the Basque Country, Navarra and Catalonia; the areas bordering France.

If you are feeding more people, allow one large duck breast to three people, you should be safe, especially if you serve this as we do with lentils and some black rice from the Veneto, *riso di Venere*.

❊ Preheat the oven to 200ºC/400ºF/gas mark 6. Score the fat side of the duck breasts with a sharp knife and rub with salt, pepper and honey. Place on a baking tray and roast for 15–20 minutes. Remove from the oven and place on a board. Allow to sit for 10 minutes.

❊ Meanwhile, drain the fat from the baking tray (reserve it for cooking) and place the tray over a medium-low heat. Tip in the orange juice, zest and sherry.

❊ Thicken with the cornflour mixed to a paste with some of the duck fat, if desired, in which case cook the sauce until thick.

❊ Slice the duck, place it on a serving dish and pour the sauce over.

Pollo Marroquí con aceitunas y limón

Moroccan chicken with olives and preserved lemon

Serves 10

2 chickens (corn-fed, if possible), with livers, and gizzards if available

300ml (½ pint) olive oil

1 tsp ground ginger, or grated root ginger

1 cinnamon stick

½ tsp salt

pinch of saffron strands

leaves from 1 bunch of coriander, finely chopped

leaves from 1 bunch of flat-leaf parsley, finely chopped, plus more to serve

3 sweet white onions, sliced

1 tomato, grated

4–6 potatoes, cut into chunks

4 garlic cloves, crushed

16 green olives

zest of ½ preserved lemon, flesh and pith removed, cut in thin julienne strips

lemon wedges, to serve

Many North African culinary traditions have left their mark in Andalusia, particularily in the provinces of Córdoba and Granada where local recipes combine unusual spices and herbs and mix the savoury with the sweet.

This recipe is in fact from Morocco, but all the ingredients come easily to hand in southern Spain. Every winter, when lemons are plentiful, we salt them and pack them in olive oil (see page 205). They stay a few days in the sun, then live on a shelf in our warm kitchen. The preserved lemons are ready to use within a couple of months and are a stunning, translucent yellow.

The Aracena mountains are one of the few areas of Andalusia where coriander is used in cooking and bunches of it are readily available in the local markets.

Put all the ingredients except the olives, preserved lemon zest and lemon wedges in a large, deep saucepan and pour in 1.2 litres (2 pints) of water. Place over a medium heat and bring to the boil, then reduce to a simmer and cook for 40–50 minutes. Remove the chickens with their livers and gizzards (if using) and the potatoes and keep them warm. Boil the sauce to reduce it.

Pound the livers (if using) in a mortar and stir them into the sauce. Cut up the chicken into serving-sized pieces, place it in a warmed serving dish with the potatoes and cover with the sauce.

Decorate the dish with the olives and preserved lemon zest (and the chicken gizzards, if using), add the lemon wedges, then sprinkle with parsley. Serve with a salad of roasted, skinned red peppers and some crusty bread.

Carne
Meat

In our mountains, as in much of the Spanish interior, meat plays an important role on any restaurant menu. Even though people will only eat meat at home perhaps once or twice a week, eating out is an occasion for celebration and an overabundance of meat is likely to appear on your plate; often enough of it for two people!

We can obtain most kinds of free-range farmed meat and chicken is ubiquitous, but beef is eaten more in the coastal north where the rich pastures of Galicia, Asturias, Cantabria and the Basque Country are perfect for raising cattle. The province of León is famous for its dried beef, *cecina*, which is akin to Italian *bresaola* or Swiss *bündnerfleisch*. Central Spain, in particular Castile, specialises in lamb, while our corner of the country is Iberian pork territory.

Of course this is to type-cast the regions. Segovia's suckling pigs are to be found in the heart of 'lamb land', while down here we can get excellent organic Retinto beef from the Dehesa de San Francisco in Santa Olalla, about 30 minutes away. There is also very good beef raised in the damp green coastal area in the south of Cádiz province.

Many Spaniards are also very fond of game, both large and small, so we often meet with rabbit, partridge and hares, along with red deer and wild boar. Game habitat is found all over Spain – wherever there are low mountains covered in Mediterranean scrub – and here too you will find herds of goats, the landscape artists in areas where man is fighting nature and forest fires. Goats keep nature in check and are generous with their milk and their meat.

One of our Iberian pigs, happy with the kitchen scraps. During summer and early autumn we supplement the pigs' foraging with surplus vegetables from the orchard, windfall fruit and leftover bread

Conejo con mostaza y nata
Rabbit with cream and mustard

Serves 6–8

2 large sweet white onions, finely sliced

olive oil

plain flour

salt and freshly ground black pepper

2 rabbits, jointed by the butcher

200ml (7fl oz) white wine

2 garlic cloves, finely chopped

2 tsp wholegrain mustard

600ml (1 pint) double cream

This is an escapee from France: a good solid country recipe which I make no excuses for putting in my book, because it is so delicious! The dish is simplicity itself and, if you are feeling greedy – as you might when contemplating it – then go the whole hog and serve it with Chestnut and potato purée (see right).

We honeymooned in Ireland, as Sam wanted me to get to know his country of birth and I had never been there. We were advised that Inishbofin was a 'must'. Lying off the coast of County Galway, in those days it was reached by trawler. We rented a cottage on the island and our neighbour, Pat Tierny, would come out of an evening and smoke on the doorstep as he watched the light change.

One evening his dog followed us as we went to fish for mackerel. We had not gone a mile when a rabbit started up from beneath our feet. Pat's dog caught it and I killed it with a sharp rabbit punch, took it down to the shore and there, on the white, sandy beach, skinned it with my Swiss Army pen knife. I had been taught by my father that whatever you killed you ate, so I washed it in the sea and we took it home with a couple of mackerel for Pat. I cooked the rabbit in butter, wild herbs off the hill and the juice of a lemon we had brought with us for gins and tonic; 'I knew I'd married the perfect woman,' said Sam as we tucked in to our dinner, 'but this is impressive'. He knew I would survive the wilds of Spain.

✻ Preheat the oven to 160ºC/325ºF/gas mark 3. Soften the onions in a little olive oil in a large casserole dish.

✻ Place the flour in a shallow dish and season it well. Dip the rabbit joints in the seasoned flour and fry, in batches, in a little oil in a frying pan until golden. As they are gilded, place the rabbit pieces in the casserole dish with the onions. Deglaze the frying pan with the white wine, then pour it over the rabbit.

THE BUENVINO COOKBOOK

✻ Add all the other ingredients, stir so the onion and rabbit are all distributed in the juices and put on a tightly fitting lid. Place in the oven and roast for 90 minutes. Before serving, pour the sauce into a saucepan, removing the rabbit and keeping it warm. Boil the sauce to reduce and thicken it, then tip it back over the rabbit and serve.

Chestnut and potato purée

Serves 10–12

500g (1lb 2oz) peeled chestnuts

500ml (18fl oz) chicken stock, plus more if needed

500g (1lb 2oz) potatoes

60g (2oz) unsalted butter

milk, to thin the purée, if needed

salt and freshly ground black pepper

I remember roasting chestnuts on the fire in Scotland in the Christmas holidays; there's a feeling of home that comes with them, images of firelight fused with a syrupy nostalgia for childhood and the anticipation of Christmas, perhaps.

Most years we gather about 2,000kg (4,400lb) of chestnuts on the farm. It's an awful lot. A quick polish and the shiny nuts are ready to be bagged up for the supermarkets, or exported to Brazil and North America. We keep a 50kg (110lb) bag for our own use and many dark evenings are spent in the kitchen pricking, boiling, peeling and freezing so we have nuts for use throughout the year.

Chestnuts are satisfyingly starchy and, once cooked, have the sweetness of a sweet potato. Any leftovers of this purée make excellent soup, with the addition of a little more chicken stock.

✻ Simmer the chestnuts in stock to cover until they are very tender and have absorbed most of the liquid. Purée in a blender, adding enough of their cooking liquor to make a thin purée.

✻ Meanwhile, peel the potatoes, boil and mash them. Combine with the chestnut purée and warm gently, stirring in the butter and more stock or milk, if needed; enough to keep it light. Season well.

Conejo con espinaca y albaricoques
Rabbit, spinach and apricots

Serves 4–6

75g (2½oz) dried apricots

450g (1lb) spinach leaves, coarse stalks removed

80g (2¾oz) unsalted butter

4 tbsp extra virgin olive oil

2 sweet white onions, finely chopped

2 garlic cloves, very finely chopped or crushed

salt and freshly ground black pepper, plus 1 tsp peppercorns

4 rabbit leg portions, each weighing about 175g (6oz), thigh bones removed by the butcher

100ml (3½fl oz) dry fino or oloroso sherry

leaves from 6 sprigs of tarragon, stalks reserved

200ml (7fl oz) strong home-made chicken stock

100ml (3½fl oz) double cream

¼ tsp smoked hot paprika (pimientón picante de la Vera)

1 tsp smoked sweet paprika (pimientón dulce de la Vera)

freshly grated nutmeg

The subtle apricot, with its perfumed balance of sweetness and acidity, is a perfect foil for the delicate flesh of the rabbit. This recipe is a little more elaborate than the others I have given in this book, so take your time and save it for special occasions.

When we were building Buenvino, it was December and we would shortly be travelling to Scotland for Christmas. We'd been celebrating our eldest child Jago's first birthday quietly, with a small cake and one candle. Some neighbours had joined us when their father arrived with a gift for Jago. A live rabbit! Jago cuddled it for a moment, and I turned to Carlos anxiously. Would he be able to look after the rabbit until we got back from Scotland? 'Oh it's not a pet, it's for eating,' he exclaimed, grabbing the rabbit and giving it a swift death blow.

'How kind,' we murmured. Luckily Jago seemed unperturbed. This must be how cavemen's children learned to hunt, I thought...

❊ Put the dried apricots in a bowl, cover with cold water and set aside to soak for 30 minutes.

❊ Blanch the spinach leaves in boiling water for 30 seconds, drain and refresh in iced water. Drain again and squeeze out all the excess water. Chop one-third of the spinach; leave the remainder as whole leaves.

❊ Heat 20g (¾oz) of the butter and half the oil in a small pan over a low heat and cook half the onions until soft. Add half the garlic and cook for one minute longer. Set aside to cool.

❊ Preheat the oven to 180ºC/350ºF/gas mark 4. Drain the apricots and finely chop. Combine the apricots and the cooked onion and garlic mixture with the spinach in a bowl and season.

❊ Fill the pocket in each rabbit thigh with the spinach mixture, packing it in loosely. There will be some left over; we will use it later. Sew up the opening or close it with wooden cocktail sticks.

❊ Heat a roasting pan over a medium heat and add the remaining oil. Arrange the rabbit portions in the pan and transfer to the oven. Roast for 20–25 minutes. Crush the peppercorns in a mortar.

✳ Remove the rabbit portions from the pan and set aside in a warm place. Pour all the fat from the pan. Put the pan over a low heat and add 20g (¾oz) of the remaining butter. Cook the rest of the onions until soft, stirring often. Add the remaining garlic and cook for one minute longer. Stir in the sherry and crushed peppercorns, increase the heat and bring to the boil. Add the tarragon stalks and boil until the sherry has reduced by three-quarters. Stir in the stock, cream and paprikas and return to the boil, simmering until the sauce thickens. Strain through a sieve, pressing on the vegetables and seasonings to extract flavour and liquid. Chop the tarragon leaves and stir them in. Adjust the seasoning and keep warm.

✳ Heat the remaining butter and add the remaining leftover spinach stuffing mixture. Toss until heated through, seasoning with nutmeg, salt and pepper.

✳ Remove the string or cocktail sticks from the rabbit and cut each stuffed portion into quarters. Arrange on warmed plates with the extra stuffing and pour the sauce over. Serve with sautéed potatoes.

Solomillo de cerdo ibérico con pimientos
Iberian pork fillets with red peppers

Serves 8–10

2 red peppers, roasted, peeled and sliced (see page 134), or, ideally, canned *pimiento del piquillo*

4 garlic cloves, finely sliced

1 tbsp olive oil

salt and freshly ground black pepper

5 pork fillets (Iberian if you can get it; it is infinitely superior to white pork)

200ml (7fl oz) dry oloroso sherry

The Sierra de Aracena is separated from the main body of the Sierra Morena by the North-South trunk road known as La Ruta de la Plata (the silver route). This long-established road links Seville, via Extremadura, with Oviedo on the north coast of Spain. As far north as Salamanca, many of the farms on either side are rolling expanses of *dehesa*: meadows where wild spring flowers and pasture are shaded by great evergreen oak trees. These are the *encinas* which provide the acorns on which the famous Iberian pigs are fed. Around Aracena, the pigs' autumn diet is supplemented with chestnuts. After our nuts are harvested, the pigs are let loose into the chestnut groves to forage for leftovers.

❋ If you are using the excellent Spanish canned *pimientos del piquillo*, drain them, cut them open and slice into strips. Fry the garlic and the peppers in the olive oil until soft and translucent. Remove from the pan with a slotted spoon and set aside.

❋ Salt and pepper the pork fillets, then fry them one by one in the hot oil, until browned all over. Put on a board and allow to rest for a few minutes before slicing them into noisettes, each about a finger thick. Iberian pork is eaten pink, so there should be a little blood running out; don't worry, Iberian pork meat should be treated like beef.

❋ Deglaze the pan with the sherry, then return the pork and peppers with any of their juices. Reheat everything, put into a warmed serving dish and take to the table. We like to drink a good strong Ribera del Guadiana wine from Extremadura with this, and you could accompany the meat with green beans, or roast tomatoes, and sautéed potatoes.

A rich version of Iberian pork fillets with red peppers, with double cream added to the sauce before serving

THE BUENVINO COOKBOOK

Solomillo de cerdo ibérico con salsa de Cabrales
Iberian pork fillets with Cabrales sauce

Serves 8–10

2 tbsp olive oil

25g (1oz) unsalted butter

5 pork fillets (Iberian if you can get it; it is infinitely superior to white pork)

salt and freshly ground black pepper

2 tbsp Spanish brandy

150ml (5fl oz) double cream

75g (2¾oz) Cabrales or other creamy blue cheese, crumbled

handful of flat-leaf parsley leaves, chopped

Cabrales is a blue cheese from the village of that name in Asturias. It is fine and creamy and usually made from a combination of sheep's and cow's milk.

❋ Heat the oil and butter in a heavy-based frying pan over a high heat. Open out the pork fillets by cutting them lengthways part way in two (don't cut them right through). Spread them out flat and season them. Fry them until cooked, the length of time varies according to size but they should be browned on the outside and pink on the inside. Remove and keep warm while the meat rests.

❋ Reduce the heat under the pan and add the brandy, stirring up all the juices. Add the cream and boil to reduce it a little. Add the crumbled cheese and mash into the sauce with the back of a spoon.

❋ Taste for seasoning. Serve the sauce in a small sauce boat, or poured over the pork, sprinkled with the parsley.

THE BUENVINO COOKBOOK

astilla	1'95
spinazo	2'95
engua	2'95
iñones	1'80
Higado	1'80
anceta	2'95
Papada	2'50
ella	1'2
ocino de Lomo	
orazón	0'9
Pulmón	
esada	1'0
morro	
	2'50

Presa	13'0
Solomillo	13'90
Lomo	13'90
Carrillera	6'90
Castañetas	7'21
Secretos	13'50
Pluma	13'80
Lagarto	7'20
Chuleta de Lomo	10'60
Cabeza de Lomo 2ª	5'99
Secreto de Papada	4'50
Magro de Aporte	

Cocido Andaluz o puchero
Chickpea and meat stew

Serves 12–15

600g (1lb 5oz) dried chickpeas

1 tsp bicarbonate of soda

2 sweet white onions, sliced

6 garlic cloves

150ml (5fl oz) olive oil

400g (14oz) meat (beef, pork, chicken or game), in one piece

200g (7oz) pancetta, in one piece

1 ham bone

salt and freshly ground black pepper

250g (9oz) ripe tomatoes, skinned and chopped (see page 96)

1 courgette, chopped

250g (9oz) green beans

3 potatoes, peeled and halved

2 tsp smoked sweet paprika (pimientón dulce de la Vera)

This is a perfect dish for Aga cooks, as it has to cook slowly for four hours, with only the occasional intervention to add ingredients to the stockpot.

This recipe will show you the basic principles behind cooking any sort of *puchero*, a stew made from fresh and salt meats, chickpeas and vegetables. Sometimes chorizo and black pudding are added. The smoky flavour of bacon or a ham bone add richness to the stock, which is eaten first as a soup. Don't worry too much about exact quantities; this is an informal hotchpotch of a dish.

At the Finca we enjoy this stew when we have a group of neighbours around for a pig killing. We put in the spare ribs and backbone of the pig for flavour, and we are nourished as we work preparing the marinades for the chorizo and salchichón and curing the hams ready for air-drying.

When we are gathered around the table for lunch at a pig killing, we have jugs filled with a simple white wine from the Cooperative at La Palma del Condado. This gets passed around the table like a 'loving cup' and we all end up rather merry. Usually the men, who have started the day at sun-up with anis and brandy, are worse for wear, so the women are left to do the clearing up, but I'm famous for being fierce and standing no nonsense: there's still so much work to be done in the afternoon, drunk or not.

Luckily on day two there is not much knife work involved in the afternoon! It is *puchero* day, and after lunch we fill the sausage skins for chorizo and salchichón, and dip the freshly made morcilla into cauldrons of simmering water for five minutes before hanging them from hooks in the shed.

The night before

❉ Put the chickpeas in a large bowl with the bicarbonate of soda and cover with plenty of water, as they will swell. Leave overnight.

Hour 1

❉ Soften the onions and garlic in the olive oil in a large pan, big enough to take all the ingredients. Add the drained chickpeas, cover with boiling water and establish a simmer. Let them cook for one hour, skimming the surface of foam every now and again.

Hours 2 and 3

✤ Add the meat, pancetta and ham bone to the pan and simmer for two further hours. Season carefully to taste, remembering that the ham bone and bacon are both salty.

Hour 4

✤ Add the tomatoes, courgette, green beans, potatoes and paprika and leave to cook for a final hour.

Ready!

✤ If the mixture is not thick enough, remove some of the chickpeas, purée them in a blender, return to the pan and cook for a little longer. Remove the meat and cut it into chunks. Serve the chickpeas in warmed deep soup plates with bread. Serve the meat on a separate plate, or all at the same time, it's up to you. This dish is wonderfully versatile. Sometimes we omit the paprika and throw in a large bunch of mint leaves instead, to make a spring version. Or we add morcilla and chorizo slices. And any leftovers can be puréed, thickened with bechamel and made into excellent croquettes.

A version of Chickpea and meat stew with added chorizo and morcilla

Cuscús de carne, castañas y peras
Couscous with beef, chestnut and pear tagine

Serves 8–10

For the tagine

325g (11½oz) fresh chestnuts, or 250g (9oz) peeled vacuum-packed chestnuts

1.1kg (2lb 8oz) braising beef

salt and freshly ground black pepper

175ml (6fl oz) dry white wine

beef stock, if needed (optional)

2 firm pears, such as Conference, quartered, or 8 quarters of Pears in syrup (see page 200)

For the picada

5 tbsp olive oil

6 almonds

25g (1oz) stale white country bread, crusts removed

1 garlic clove, finely chopped

For the couscous

500g packet of couscous

a little unsalted butter

Local beef mainly comes from the sturdy Retinto cattle. Ancestors of Texan cattle, it's a breed that can stand the lengthy Spanish summer drought, feeding on scrubby bushes long after the spring grass has been eaten. The cattle begin to put on weight again when the first rains fall in late October. In a week or two the shy flush of green winter pasture, known as the *otoñal*, appears.

This dish is typically at its best in late autumn when the last tomatoes have refused to ripen, the chestnuts and the pears have been harvested and the first weeks of autumn rain have started to green up the pasture meadows.

We often serve this with Warm green tomato relish (see right).

If using fresh chestnuts, make a slit in each nut and simmer in water for about 20 minutes, then peel them. There is a knack to this, and you'll soon get it.

For the picada, heat the oil in a wide casserole and fry the almonds, bread and garlic for the picada, in turn, until a pale gold, then remove with a slotted spoon and set aside.

Cut the beef into finger-width slices. Salt and pepper each strip lightly and fry in the oil, in batches, until coloured all over. (Never put in too many pieces at once, or they will stew rather than fry. You need the pan to remain hot.) Now return all the meat to the pan along with the wine and 175ml (6fl oz) of water.

Cover and braise gently for about 45 minutes, checking from time to time that there is enough liquid.

Prepare the sauce. Grind up the almonds, bread and garlic in a mortar and pestle. Stir in some of the meat juices, then stir the picada into the pan and allow the tagine to thicken.

Check that the meat is properly cooked with a good strong gravy; season if required and add stock or water if the sauce is too thick. Add the chestnuts and the pears to the casserole and heat through.

Meanwhile, put the couscous into a heatproof bowl, dot with butter and pour over boiling water (the quantities should be two measures of couscous to three measures of water). Allow to absorb for five minutes. After a few minutes, break up the couscous with a fork. If there are still some lumps, crumble them up with your fingertips, making sure not to burn yourself.

Spoon the beef and sauce over the couscous in a pretty dish and bring directly to the table with warmed soup bowls for your guests.

Warm green tomato relish

Serves 8–10 as a relish

2–3 tbsp olive oil

500g green tomatoes, sliced

salt and freshly ground black pepper

1 tsp plain flour

pinch of freshly ground cumin

Our Sierra de Aracena climate is cooler than that of the plains of Andalusia and, as a result, our tomato crop ripens at almost the same time as it would in northern Europe. Once we have harvested and bottled the ripe tomatoes, we are left with many green fruits. The sun has slipped between the hills to the south of our orchards, and these last tomatoes will never ripen.

The big, pale green beef tomatoes are often served in the tapas bars of Aracena and Los Marines as a snack. They are cooked in oil with cumin and are excellent served with fresh bread and manchego cheese. We cook them in the same way and use them as a side dish.

Put the olive oil in a pan to heat.

Season the green tomatoes with salt and pepper. Mix the flour and cumin on a plate and dip the tomato slices in this.

Fry the tomatoes in the oil until tender. They will splutter and need a bit of cooking to soften up.

Serve warm with the beef, chestnut and pear tagine.

Caldereta de chivito con pimientones morrones
Kid with red peppers and mint

Serves 4

900g (2lb) kid leg meat, cut into cubes

salt and freshly ground black pepper

4 red peppers

4 tbsp olive oil

3 garlic cloves, finely sliced

1 large sweet white onion, finely chopped

200g (7oz) Serrano ham, finely chopped

5 large tomatoes, grated, or 400g can of tomatoes

1 tbsp smoked sweet paprika (pimientón dulce de la Vera)

300ml (½ pint) dry white wine (we use local Huelva or Cádiz wines)

1 tbsp chopped mint leaves

Wild, sparsely inhabited country lies at the outer reaches of the Sierra de Aracena and further east through the 400km (250 mile) length of the Sierra Morena (the black mountains).

Seen from afar, it's easy to understand the name. The uncultivated ground is colonised and darkly coloured by the greeny-black *monte bajo*, the Spanish equivalent of the French *maquis*. Away from the olive groves, the *dehesa* and the chestnut forests, you'll find a great wilderness covered in a mixture of aromatic Mediterranean scrub: rosemary, cistus, broom, gorse and myrtle. It teems with red deer, wild boar, pockets of mouflon, rabbits and hares, all hunted in the autumn and winter months.

In spring, the *Cistus ladaniferus*, or gum rock rose, opens its papery blooms and the hills seem to be covered in snow. It all looks wonderful, but these resinous plants are rampant, present a fire hazard and need to be dominated.

Traditionally the hills have been grazed by large flocks of free-range goats attended by lonely and self-sufficient goatherds. Over the past half-century these people have become scarce. A new generation of better informed, better educated young people aspire at least to a motorbike, a car and a Friday night of partying, or else move on to the cities for further education and, hopefully, better-paid work.

In our area of smaller farms, the owners of the goats will tend them morning and night, letting them out of their pens in the morning, and milking them in the evening during the spring, when the young kids have been weaned. Goats will always be a part both of the land management scheme and of the local diet. Female kids are raised up to become mothers and milk producers, while male kids are usually killed at a few months for the table. If you cannot get hold of kid, you could use young lamb instead.

This is a great spring dish to be eaten in the middle of the day out of doors, when the air is still cool, the countryside green and the sun brilliant. Burst open some potatoes baked in wood ash in an open fire and spoon the kid over them. We would suggest a bottle of rosado from Catalonia or the Somontano in Aragon where fine varietal wines are made, or else a clarete from the Rioja Alta.

cont...

THE BUENVINO COOKBOOK

✳ Season the kid with salt and pepper. Roast the peppers under a preheated grill, or over a gas flame, turning, until the skins are black and flaking. Put them into a paper bag or wrap them in greaseproof paper and leave them to cool; this makes them easier to peel. When cool, peel, deseed and slice into broad strips.

✳ Heat the oil in a large flameproof casserole. Add the kid, a handful at a time, and brown over a fairly high heat. Remove with a slotted spoon and repeat with the next handful, until all is browned. Return all the meat to the pan, add the garlic, onion and ham and sauté for a few minutes, then throw in the peppers and the tomatoes. Sprinkle over the paprika, stir it all well and then add the wine with 300ml (½ pint) of water. Put on the lid and cook slowly for about one and a quarter hours.

✳ Add the mint. Cook for a further 15–30 minutes; the meat should be completely tender. Serve with baked potatoes.

Rabo de toro serrano
Mountain-style oxtail

Serves 6–8

60g (2oz) pork dripping, or lard, plus more for the croutons

1 oxtail, cut up by the butcher

125g (4½oz) carrots, finely chopped

175g (6oz) sweet white onions, finely chopped

40g (1½oz) plain flour

1 litre (1¾ pints) dry white wine

herbs (oregano, thyme and bay) tied together in a bouquet garni

salt and freshly ground black pepper

250g (9oz) salted *tocino*, cubed, or *tacos de jamón* (the drier pieces of a ham which are used for flavouring), or diced bacon if you can't get either of these

cont.

This is the Spanish way with oxtail. It's a hearty winter dish which we often enjoy at José Vicente's restaurant in Aracena when the winter rains are lashing down and we have no clients, but plenty of time to meet local friends around the lunch table.

It's an easy dish to prepare, but also one for a long weekend in the country since it's best to cook the oxtail, leave it in the fridge overnight to gain flavour, then remove the solidified fat the following day before adding the final touches.

Day 1

✳ Preheat the oven to 180ºC/350ºF/gas mark 4.

✳ Heat the pork dripping in a heavy-based pan that has a lid, add the pieces of oxtail and brown gently over a medium heat, turning. Add the carrots and onions and, when fairly browned, sprinkle in the flour, stir well and cook together for a few minutes, allowing the mixture to take on some colour. Add the wine little by little, stirring to amalgamate the gravy, then add the bouquet garni and season. Bring to the boil, cover and put in the oven for three hours. Cover, cool and refrigerate.

250g (9oz) salchichón or saucisson sec, cut into 3cm (generous 1in) slices

450g (1lb) fresh chestnuts , peeled (see page 130), or vacuum-packed peeled chestnuts

1 celery stick, finely chopped

2 slices of brown bread, cut into cubes

Day 2

✳ Fry the *tocino* or *tacos de jamón* and the sausages very gently in their own fat for about two minutes. Cook the chestnuts in lightly salted water with the celery for 20 minutes, then drain.

✳ Remove the fat from the top of the oxtail stew and reheat the stew gently. Place it in a serving dish with the celery, chestnuts, *tocino* or *tacos de jamón* and sausages.

✳ Meanwhile, fry the bread in more pork dripping until golden and crispy. Serve with the oxtail.

Cordero con salsa de chocolate
Roast lamb with chocolate

Serves 8

2kg (4lb 8oz) leg of lamb, unboned weight, boned by the butcher

salt and freshly ground black pepper

2–4 garlic cloves, plus more to roast around the lamb

handful of rosemary leaves, plus more sprigs for the oven dish

150ml (5fl oz) olive oil, plus more for the oven dish

300ml (½ pint) strong 'plunger', or French press, coffee

115g (4oz) dark (70% cocoa solids) chocolate

This recipe is a combination of two influences: Nordic and Mediterranean. For many years we used a delicious Scandinavian recipe for cooking lamb in coffee, then making a gravy with redcurrants and cream.

Here we go Spanish with the addition of chocolate, garlic and rosemary. You will be surprised by the contented marriage between the strong flavours of lamb, chocolate and garlic.

❋ Preheat the oven to 200ºC/400ºF/gas mark 6.

❋ Open the meat out, skin side down. Sprinkle with salt and rub well all over. Grind on some black pepper, then, in a mini food processor, grind up the garlic and rosemary until you have a pungent paste. Spread this over the lamb. Roll it together again and place it skin side up into a well-oiled deep flameproof oven dish, then throw in a small handful of garlic cloves and some rosemary sprigs. Pour on the 150ml (5fl oz) olive oil and sprinkle the meat with salt and pepper.

❋ Pour the coffee into the oven dish around the meat, place in the middle of the hot oven and roast, allowing 15 minutes for every 450g (1lb) of weight. When the meat is cooked, remove it from the oven dish and place it on a carving board to rest.

❋ Tip or spoon the surplus fat and oil out of the oven dish. Put the dish over a low gas flame and break in the chocolate, stirring constantly. The sauce will thicken and turn dark brown in colour.

❋ When the meat has rested, slice it carefully on to a warmed dish, cover with the sauce and serve. A good hearty Cariñena red would be ideal with this.

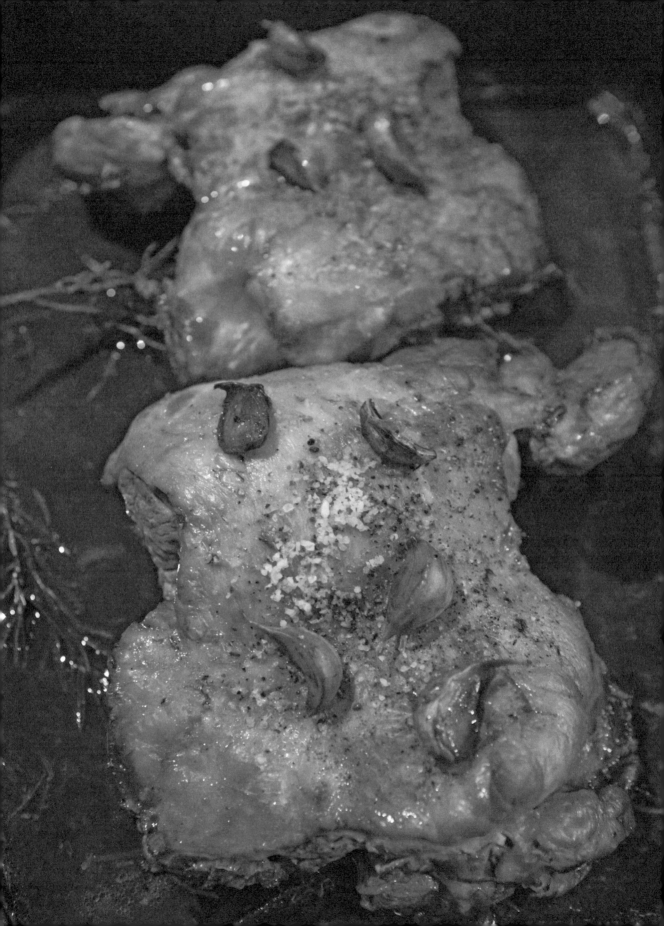

Cordero con berenjenas
Lamb with aubergines

Serves 8

For the tagine

1.5kg (3lb 5oz) lamb, cut into pieces

½ tsp salt

1 tsp freshly ground black pepper

½ tsp saffron strands

2 sweet white onions, sliced

2 garlic cloves, crushed

120ml (4fl oz) olive oil

2 tomatoes, grated (skins discarded)

leaves from 1 large bunch of flat-leaf parsley, chopped

For the aubergines

2kg (4lb 8oz) aubergines

2 egg whites

½ tsp salt

1 tbsp white wine vinegar

2 tbsp olive oil, plus more if needed

This is another Moroccan tagine dish, and the stems and florets of the aubergines lend it a very distinct flavour which reminds us always of a wedding in Fez, where we first ate it. We will never forget the kind hospitality of our hosts, nor how we were perched rather awkwardly on low cushions, dressed in our finery (Sam in suit and tie), as we did our best, after duly washing our hands in rose water, to tuck into the delicious, subtle food without making too much of a mess of ourselves. Later, we danced in circles, holding hands with other guests as we learned to let our hips swivel dramatically. The immobile bride and groom sat in high splendour, on heaps of metallic lurex cushions, their hands joined ceremonially by an assistant.

Put all the ingredients for the tagine, except the tomatoes and parsley, into a pan with 1.7 litres (3 pints) of water and bring to the boil. Reduce the heat to a simmer, cover and cook for one hour.

Meanwhile, remove the stems and leaflets from the aubergines and reserve them on a plate. Slice the aubergines into circles.

Mix together the egg whites, salt and vinegar in a shallow bowl. Dip the aubergine slices into the egg white mixture, to prevent them from drinking up too much oil, then fry them, in batches, in the 2 tbsp of hot oil until tender all the way through. Add more oil as you think it is needed. Drain them on kitchen paper, then crush them with a fork on a plate while still hot.

Remove the meat from the tagine and keep it warm. Put the aubergine purée on top of the meat.

Add the stems and florets from the aubergines to the tagine with the tomatoes and parsley. Bring the sauce to the boil, then reduce the heat to a simmer and allow it to thicken slightly. Pour the sauce back over the meat. Serve at once with couscous (see pages 130–131).

Ensaladas
Salads

The most basic salad eaten in Andalusia is one of lettuce (generally cos lettuce), tomato and sweet onion, dressed quite simply with olive oil and vinegar. No matter how hard I try, it's impossible to reproduce the flavour of the salads one is given at roadside inns or restaurants in town, and I suspect their unique, refreshing quality lies in the fact that the lettuce has been washed and chilled – and comes to the table without having been throughly rinsed – so that a little water dilutes the vinegar. The olive oil is always good and sometimes mint leaves have been chopped into the salad, or thin-skinned frying peppers cut into slim rings to add extra crunch.

If you are not careful to ask for a 'simple salad', your lettuce will be concealed beneath layers of droopy canned asparagus, sweetcorn and slivers of carrot or beetroot preserved in vinegar. Better to stick to the alternatives in this chapter, one of my favourites being a picadillo, which is every bit as refreshing as a well-made gazpacho.

Salud, who sells vegetables in her mother's shop in Aracena

Ensalada de tomates con almendras
Moroccan tomato and almond salad

Serves 8

For the salad

4–5 sweet ripe beef tomatoes

1 large sweet white onion, if possible, or a sweet red onion

a little olive oil

large fistful of whole blanched almonds

salt and freshly ground black pepper

caster sugar

ground cinnamon

basil leaves, to serve

For the dressing

4 tbsp extra virgin olive oil

1 tbsp toasted argan, pumpkin, or sesame oil

1 tbsp sherry vinegar, or good strong red wine vinegar

1 tsp English mustard powder

pinch of caster sugar

pinch of salt

We first came across this delicious combination when driving around Morocco in the mid-1980s. We had travelled up the Ourika valley and visited small argan oil producers. We brought several plastic mineral water bottles home to Spain, each filled with the nut-brown oil pressed from roasted argan nuts.

In Morocco, or when we have just returned from travelling there, we would use toasted argan oil in the dressing for this salad; otherwise we use toasted pumpkin or sesame oils.

❊ Slice the tomatoes across into thinnish discs. Slice the onion thinly and break the slices into rings.

❊ Put some olive oil into a small pan and throw in the almonds. Toast them gently, stirring from time to time so they are evenly browned. Drain them on kitchen paper and allow to cool a little.

❊ Meanwhile, put a layer of tomatoes on a wide shallow dish. Sprinkle with salt and a little sugar, then drop a few onion rings over them. Now shake some cinnamon over (not a thick layer, just a dusting). Repeat until all the tomatoes and onions have been used up, ending with a layer of cinnamon-sprinkled onions. Grind some black pepper over the salad.

❊ Put the almonds on to a wooden board on a low table. Now get a wooden rolling pin and slowly, while the almonds are still warm and soft, lean down on the almonds, rolling the pin back and forth, until they are cracked. Scoop up the broken almonds and sprinkle over the tomato salad.

❊ For the dressing, emulsify all the ingredients with a hand-held blender, adding 1 tbsp of water, and spoon over the tomatoes. Add some torn basil leaves here and there and bring to the table.

A note on onions
Our onions are either brown-skinned, with white sweet flesh, or purple and equally sweet. Perhaps because they are just pulled out from the garden they are not apt to make one weep, and are not overpoweringly strong.

Andalusian picadillo

Serves 8-10

2 cucumbers, peeled and finely chopped

1 green pepper, finely chopped

1 small sweet white onion, finely chopped

extra virgin olive oil

sherry vinegar

salt

4 tomatoes

The secret of a good picadillo is to prepare it well in advance, preferably the night before, then chill it in the refrigerator so that all the flavours have a chance to come together. It's like a refreshing and chewy gazpacho, perfect for picnics on a hot day.

❋ Tip the cucumbers, pepper and onion into a bowl or a sealable plastic box.

❋ Make a vinaigrette with the oil, vinegar and salt, pour it over the vegetables and stir them up with your hand.

Right: Andalusian picadillo; Far right: Andalusian picadillo with cod's roe

THE BUENVINO COOKBOOK

※ If you are maturing the picadillo overnight to eat for lunch on the following day, it's a good idea to leave the tomatoes out until morning. The cucumber will have crisped up overnight and the vegetables will have released some juice.

※ Chop the tomatoes into smallish dice and throw them into the other vegetables. Mix gently so the tomatoes don't fall apart.

※ Traditionally this is served in a bowl in the middle of the table, everyone dipping in a spoon and using a slice of bread to catch the drips between bowl and mouth. Alternatively serve in small bowls, but this is not so convivial.

Picadillo con huevas de bacalao
Andalusian picadillo with cod's roe

This is made in the same way as the picadillo above, but is chunkier, so don't cut your vegetables so finely. Prepare a raw cod's roe by boiling it in salty water or, if you prefer, steaming it, for about 10 minutes, depending on size. Allow it to cool, then skin the roe, devein it and slice into chunks, adding it to the picadillo with the tomatoes. You can also buy canned cooked cod's roe for this dish, though the texture is not quite as good as fresh.

Picadillo con papas
Andalusian picadillo with potato

This variation adds diced boiled potatoes. Before putting the dish into the fridge overnight, mix in just-cooked, still-warm potatoes, so they absorb the vinaigrette as the salad matures.

Ensalada Marroquí de zanahorias
Moroccan carrot salad

Cook about 10 peeled carrots in boiling salted water until tender. Drain in a colander. When cool enough to handle, slice into thin circles and return to the pan with a little olive oil, 1 large tbsp of honey, the juice of ½ lemon and 1 tsp ground cumin. Place over a low heat and mix well. Put in a dish and allow to cool.

Taste for seasoning and add salt and pepper if required. Toast 1 tsp each of cumin and coriander seeds in a dry pan. Toss these over the carrots. Chop some parsley finely and sprinkle over the dish. Before serving, drizzle some more olive oil over the salad to give it a shine.

Pimiento frito con ajo
Fried green peppers with garlic

There is a variety of green pepper which is long and thin-skinned and which we use for frying, much as we would do with the Fried Padrón peppers which we serve for tapas (see page 40).

To make the dish, gently fry thin-skinned green peppers whole in olive oil, with some whole garlic cloves in their skins. When the peppers are translucent and floppy, they are ready.

Place them on a flattish serving dish, scatter the garlic around, sprinkle with sea salt and, if you wish, pour over a mustardy vinaigrette.

Ensalada de calabacín
Courgette salad

Serves 8

500g (1lb 2oz) courgettes

olive oil

sea salt

Basil oil (see page 211)

sherry vinegar

handful of finely chopped garlic chives

We often have a surplus of courgettes, particularly in the early summer when they are rampant and liable to take over the whole vegetable garden. This is a delicious and simple way to use them.

✲ Slice the courgettes finely, then put them in a basin with a little olive oil and stir them round.

✲ Heat a heavy-based ridged grill pan. With a pair of tongs, grill the courgette slices until browned on both sides, then pick them up with the tongs and place them on a serving dish. When all are done, sprinkle with sea salt, then dress with basil oil and sherry vinegar. Sprinkle with the garlic chives to serve.

Pisto
Ratatouille

Serves 8

1 red pepper

1 green pepper

1kg (2lb 4oz) ripe tomatoes

150ml (5fl oz) olive oil

½ star anise

1 aubergine, finely chopped

3 courgettes, finely chopped

3 garlic cloves, finely sliced

1 large sweet white or red onion, finely chopped

3 tbsp honey

salt and freshly ground black pepper

I've included this Spanish version of a ratatouille in the salad section as we often dress it, once cold, with vinaigrette and serve it as one of many salad dishes for a summer lunch. And sometimes we cook eggs in a small terracotta dish of this, as in the photo, for a simple starter of *huevos con pisto*.

We make this orientalised version of a Spanish pisto as we were shown by our friend Henry Anderson, who cooks on oil and gas tankers, and invited us on board for dinner in the Port of Huelva. If you are not fond of the flavour of star anise, then substitute a bay leaf, or some thyme or oregano, for a more classical version.

※ Roast the peppers over an open gas flame until blistered, then place them in a paper bag to steam and loosen their skins.

※ Cut the tomatoes in half and grate them into a bowl with a coarse cheese grater. Discard the skins. If you are truly fussy about tomato seeds, you could pass the purée through a sieve at this juncture; I find it a waste of time.

※ Carefully remove the blackened skin from the peppers and throw away the cores and seeds. Finely chop the flesh.

※ Tip the olive oil into a wide non-stick pan and heat. When the oil is beginning to smoke, throw in the star anise, followed by the aubergine, the courgettes, garlic and onion. Reduce the heat and cook, stirring constantly so the vegetables do not brown. When the flavoured oil is almost absorbed by the aubergine pieces, add the tomatoes and peppers and cook on a low heat so the flavours simmer together. Check from time to time that the tomato is not burning and give it a stir. You want the tomatoes to cook through and then reduce.

※ When all is cooked, stir in the honey and season well. This is delicious and versatile; serve it hot or cold on its own, or perhaps drizzled over potatoes or cold sliced pork. Or cook eggs in it for *huevos con pisto*, as in the photograph. Or, once cold, add a little sherry vinegar to sharpen it up and serve it as a salad.

Huevos con pisto

Olive oil

Spanish olive oils have a wide variety of aromas, flavours and colours, ranging from a transparent golden tone to a deep green hue. Despite what one might think, these variations are not necessarily an indication of taste. The only way of judging an oil is to taste it.

According to government sources, Spain is the world's largest producer of olive oil, with an annual yield of between 700,000 and 1,400,000 tonnes, which represents an amazing figure somewhere between one-half to three-quarters of the world's production. Who knows if these figures are correct... all I can be sure of is that there are more olive groves planted every year in our province of Huelva, so I can only imagine the same trend is going on elsewhere in the country.

There are two basic types of olive oil exported to the United Kingdom: 'extra virgin olive oil' and, simply, 'olive oil'. Extra virgin is of the finest quality and must not exceed an acidity level of one per cent. Many Spanish extra virgin olive oils are well below this maximum.

'Olive oil' is the general name for a blend of refined and virgin oils, with a maximum of 1.5 per cent acidity.

There are five main varieties of olives for oil grown in Spain. We don't use all five constantly in our kitchen, but always have arbequina for all things salady, and picual or hojiblanca for our breakfast toast or to go into gazpacho. We're not overly fussy about using one kind or another, unless we meet something we actively dislike (some more peppery oils can catch in the throat).

The whole subject is made more complicated by the oil itself varying from producer to producer. Olive oil, like wine, is influenced by the terroir in which it is grown and has to be treated with care.

The general remarks that follow are intended as a form of guidance. Do remember that oils made by different producers – or grown on varying soils – can taste poles apart. The oils listed here are not commonly available, but it's possible to pick up these varietals in specialist shops and from specialist importers or, of course, online.

Arbequina

The aroma is reminiscent of artichokes and the smell of warm tomato plants in the sun when you brush up against them. We use this oil for dressing tender young spring vegetables, carrots or baby beets (either cooked or raw) as well as in salads, or to make scrambled eggs. This oil is at its best when uncooked, so it's great spread over toast for breakfast. Arbequina is not as generally available in our part of Spain as many of the other oils, but we appreciate its qualities, so we usually have a bottle or two in the house. The main production areas are in north eastern Spain: Tarragona, Zaragoza, Huesca and Lleida.

Cornicabra

This has a scent of ripe avocado and a balance in flavour between sweet, bitter and pungent. We use this for dressing warm potato salads, or roasted and stewed vegetables, or for garlic mayonnaise (Alioli, see page 32) as it has a strong enough flavour to play along with the crushed garlic. It's also great for marinading meat, particularly game, when mixed with a little garlic, red wine vinegar, dried oregano and salt. This variety of olive is chiefly grown in Central Spain, in Ciudad Real and Toledo provinces.

Hojiblanca

An elegant and flavoursome balance between bitter and sweet, with unexpected notes of fresh grass, chamomile and flowers. This oil is good for gently frying foods such as fish and squid. Remember, though, not to bring it to high temperatures, as that will adversely affect the flavour. Hojiblanca is also excellent for casseroles or *cocidos* and for pastries and baking. I use it when making pizza dough, when we have the wood-fired bread oven lit. It is chiefly grown in the provinces of Málaga, Córdoba and Seville.

salt flakes to eat. (We sometimes have this after dinner if we haven't made a pudding.) The main production area for this olive is in Andalusia's Jaén, Córdoba, and Granada provinces.

Picual

Fruity with a hint of freshly crushed grass, this is pungent in the mouth, with a fragrance of apples. It is used in our kitchen for salads and gazpachos. It's also one of the best for breakfast toast, either rubbed with tomato, or to which you have added a square or two of dark chocolate. Place this latter toast in a low oven until the chocolate starts to soften, then sprinkle with sea

Picudo

A light, sweet flavour, sometimes reminiscent of exotic fruits, apples and marzipan. The variety is excellent for Ajo blanco (see page 72), warm salads, stews, pastries and cake making, or in scrambled egg. It is also delicious drizzled over country bread with fresh honey. This is also a local variety to us, grown chiefly in Andalusia's Córdoba, Granada, Málaga and Jaén provinces.

Postres
Puddings

The average Spaniard eats 4kg (9lb) of sugar per year, according to the webpage of Azucarera, the largest national sugar producer... I suspect much of it stirred into cups of coffee.

If you believe that statistic, look at four packets of sugar. That's 4kg. Now look at the vast quantities of meringues and sweet cakes guzzled in every small town of Andalusia, if not every day, then at most weekends. Then think of the cities and think of the rest of Spain and the countless small *pastelerías* which are a hub in every neighbourhood.

If the statistic is correct, then there must be a host of people who never eat sugar. Where are they hiding?

When visitors drop in on us, what do they bring? Boxes of sweet cakes – very sweet cakes – almost too sweet for our northern European palates. (There are some things you cannot change, even after 30 years!)

All the sugar we buy in Spain is caster sugar, but you can use caster or granulated interchangeably in these recipes.

Seville orange soufflé

Serves 8

5 free-range eggs, separated

225g (8oz) caster sugar

2 large tbsp Seville orange marmalade

25g (scant 1oz) powdered gelatine

300ml (½ pint) double or whipping cream

whipped cream and candied peel, to serve (optional)

Praline (see overleaf, optional)

At Finca Buenvino we make marmalade every winter from the bitter Seville oranges, grown simply for adornment (and strictly not for eating) in every street in Andalusia.

Some years ago, Don Ángel, then the incumbent priest in our village, used to collect oranges from the trees in Rosal de la Frontera, the last village in Spain on the border with Portugal, then on one cold day he would turn up at our house, without warning, with a huge sack of the aromatic fruit. Jeannie fetched down the big jam pan and started to prepare what we then called 'holy marmalade'.

Nowadays Don Ángel is unable to go orange picking and we do it ourselves, much to the consternation of the people of Rosal who all rush up, tut-tutting, to explain that these are bitter, inedible oranges. I suppose it should now be called 'unholy marmalade', as Don Ángel has no hand in it! We eat it on toast for breakfast, but also use it in the following recipe. (If you can get Seville oranges during their short winter season, then do make your own, otherwise use good-quality shop-bought organic marmalade.) This soufflé is easy, quick and a great way to enjoy that sharp Seville orange flavour.

✳ Put the egg yolks and sugar into a food processor and beat until light and creamy. Add the marmalade and beat until well blended.

✳ In a small steel saucepan, sprinkle the gelatine into 3 large tbsp of cold water and allow to swell for five minutes. Place the pan over a low heat until the gelatine is fully dissolved and the liquid transparent. Don't let it get too hot, as this will damage the setting properties of the gelatine. Remove from the heat and let cool slightly, then blend into the egg yolk mixture.

✳ Beat the egg whites in a large bowl with an electric whisk until they form peaks. In another bowl, whip the cream until foamy and billowing but not stiff.

✳ Fold all the ingredients into the egg whites little by little, taking care not to beat the air out of the eggs. Tip into a pretty glass dish, or smaller dishes, and refrigerate for a minimum of three hours.

✳ Decorate with whipped cream and candied peel, or with praline.

Praline

Make this in the same way with hazelnuts instead of almonds, if you prefer. Either is great sprinkled over ice cream, or Almond semifreddo or Seville orange soufflé (see below and page 155).

Makes 225g (8oz)

115g (4oz) blanched almonds

115g (4oz) caster sugar

a little flavourless oil

We make this in small batches and keep it sealed in an airtight container. If damp gets in you will have trouble getting your praline out of the jar and, when you do, it will have lost all its charm. It's a good idea to have used it all up within a fortnight...

❋ Put the almonds and sugar in a heavy-based pan over a low heat until the sugar has melted and turned a caramel colour. Do not stir, or the whole will become crystallised and will be of no use.

❋ Carefully rotate the pan until all the nuts are covered with the brown syrup. When the nuts go pop, pour the mixture on to an oiled marble slab or into an oiled Swiss roll tin. Remember that caramel is extremely hot, so please be careful when pouring it out and *do not touch*.

❋ Leave to get cold. When the praline has set rock hard, prize it off the oiled surface or from the tin and crush it in a mortar, or in a food processor, or smash it up with a rolling pin. The texture should be quite coarse and gritty.

❋ Use what you need immediately and seal the rest into an airtight jar and store it in a dry place.

Semifrío de almendras
Almond semifreddo

Serves 8

500ml (18fl oz) double cream, well chilled

155g (5¾oz) caster sugar

5 free-range eggs, separated

about 200g (7oz) Praline (see above), plus more to serve

This recipe was given to us by Darina Allen and you will find it in her *Ballymaloe Cookery Course*, which in our house is known as 'The Grey Bible'. Although it's Italian in origin, it reminds me of a cold version of *turrón*, the almond nougat which is sold in every shop in Spain around Christmas time.

❋ Whip the cream with 100g (3½oz) of the sugar until softly whipped, then cover and keep refrigerated.

❋ Now whisk the egg yolks with the remaining sugar until light and fluffy, then fold in the sweetened whipped cream very delicately. Also fold the praline into the mousse. In turn, whisk the egg whites stiffly, then fold gently into the mousse.

❋ Divide between two cling film-lined small loaf tins, cover and freeze for a minimum of three hours, or a maximum of one month.

❋ To serve, cut the semifreddo into 1cm (½in) slices and sprinkle with a line of praline. Serve immediately on chilled plates.

Ciruelas damascenas en almíbar al orégano
Damsons in oregano syrup

Serves 8

1kg (2lb 4oz) damsons

250g (9oz) granulated sugar

1 sprig of fresh oregano or ½ tsp dried oregano

Damsons are little blue plums which ripen in Spain in late June or early July, when the wild oregano is in bloom. This refreshing cooked fruit dish can also be made with greengages or mirabelles.

❋ Rinse the damsons and place in a saucepan. Tip over 300ml (½ pint) of water. Cover and simmer gently on a low heat for about 25 minutes, until soft but still firm. Remove from the heat and carefully scoop out the fruit with a slotted spoon, reserving the liquid in the pan.

❋ Place the fruit in a non-metallic sieve over its cooking liquid and allow to drip. When the drips have mostly dried up, place the fruit in a serving dish. Any juice which continues to seep from the damsons should be added to the pan of liquid as it cooks.

❋ Tip the sugar into the liquid and allow it to dissolve over a low heat. Increase the heat and bring it to the boil, then reduce it once more to a simmer. The juice should reduce to become a syrup, but without the sugar catching and caramelising. When the liquid is a clear pink colour, throw in the sprig of oregano, or dried oregano, then remove from the heat after a few seconds. Allow the syrup to cool slowly. When it's cold, strain it over the fruit in the dish.

❋ Serve with creamed rice pudding, crème anglaise or cream.

Helado de aceite de oliva virgen
Olive oil ice cream

Serves 8

250g (9oz) caster sugar

4 free-range eggs

250ml (9fl oz) fresh-tasting green extra virgin olive oil

pinch of salt

250ml (9fl oz) whole milk

Straight from the kitchen of the British Embassy in Madrid. Use a very fruity light-coloured extra virgin olive oil; a fresh young green Arbequina would be perfect.

When Sam and I were married, our elderly aunts did not know what to give us as we were off to foreign parts, so lots of their small cheques added up and we decided, in a moment of madness (which turned out to be sanity), to invest in a fancy ice-cream maker, a Gelato Chef. A useful piece of kit to have around when the temperatures soar in a Spanish summer.

Unfortunately, when planning our purchase we had quite forgotten about the lack of electricity at our destination, so, on returning to Spain, we had to invest in a generator to run the ice-cream machine; the height of extravagance. It provided the perfect excuse for me to get out my (previously strictly rationed) hair dryer, use the food processor, or get on with the ironing... and, of course, we had a lot of ice cream!

❋ Dissolve the sugar over a medium-low heat in 125ml (4fl oz) of water in a small saucepan, then increase the heat and boil it hard for five minutes until it is transparent and there are no sugar crystals left. Let it cool.

❋ Beat the eggs, add the oil in a very thin stream while still beating, then add the cooled syrup, and finally the salt and milk.

❋ Churn in an ice-cream machine according to the manufacturer's instructions. I don't know if you could make this by hand, beating as it freezes, as I always use a machine (see recipe introduction!). A manual bucket ice-cream churn with salted ice in the outer jacket would work, though. Serve with Buttery lemon biscuits (see below).

Buttery lemon biscuits

Makes about 16

115g (4oz) unsalted butter, plus more for the trays

finely grated zest of 3 unwaxed lemons, plus a squeeze of juice

60g (2oz) caster sugar

175g (6oz) plain flour, sifted, plus more to dust

❋ Preheat the oven to 150ºC/300ºF/gas mark 2 and butter two baking trays.

❋ Cream the butter with a wooden spoon or an electric whisk until soft, add the lemon juice and sugar and beat until pale and fluffy.

❋ Now work in the flour and lemon zest and knead together lightly. Form into small balls, each about the size of a walnut. If they feel too soft because the kitchen is warm, chill them in the fridge for 20 minutes.

❋ Put them on a lightly floured table top and flatten them with your hand to about 3mm- (⅛in-) thick rough discs. The edges should crack slightly. Lift them on to the baking trays with a palette knife, prick each with a fork twice, and bake in the oven for 25 minutes until golden. (Do check that they are not burning!)

❋ Take the tray out of the oven and put the biscuits on a wire rack to cool. If you wish to serve the olive oil ice cream in a glass bowl, then stab the biscuit on its edge into the top of the ice cream.

❋ To serve on a plate, place a biscuit on to a plate first to stop the ice cream sliding about, then scoop the ice cream on top of it. Decorate with a slice of lemon, or with edible petals, if you like.

Helado de pasas con oloroso seco
Oloroso and raisin ice cream

Serves 8

50g (1¾oz) raisins

175–200ml (6–7fl oz) dry oloroso sherry

4 free-range egg yolks

6 tbsp light brown sugar

1 tsp cornflour

300ml (½ pint) whole milk

300ml (½ pint) whipping cream

1 tbsp Pedro Ximenez for each helping (optional but lovely)

You can make this ice cream with Pedro Ximenez sweet wine instead of oloroso, if you prefer; it will be more strongly flavoured and sweeter, while the oloroso version will be wonderfully subtle.

✳ Put the raisins in a pan with the oloroso and simmer gently until they have plumped up and absorbed some of the wine. Leave to cool. (Or soak the raisins in the sherry overnight without heating.)

✳ Whisk together the egg yolks, sugar and cornflour until the mixture is foamy.

✳ Heat the milk in a large, heavy-based pan to just below boiling point. Whisk the milk into the eggs, then pour back into the pan.

✳ Cook over a gentle heat, stirring with a wooden spoon, until the custard thickens enough to coat the back of the spoon and is smooth. Leave until cold, then chill.

✳ Whip the cream until it is thick and billowing, then fold it into the chilled custard.

✳ Put the mixture into an ice-cream machine and churn until thick, according to the manufacturer's instructions. You could probably make this by hand as well, pouring it into a shallow container and freezing, beating it three or four times as it freezes.

✳ Either way, spoon the nearly-finished ice cream into a freezer-proof container. Fold the raisins and their soaking liquid into the soft ice cream, then cover and freeze for two or three hours.

✳ You might like to pour some dark, rich, absurdly sweet Pedro Ximenez wine over the ice cream or, if this is too much for you, then sip a glass of Lustau's delicious East India Solera with it, served at room temperature.

Helado de castañas
Chestnut ice cream

Serves 8

1 vanilla pod

600ml (1 pint) whole milk or single cream

4 free-range egg yolks

150g (5½oz) caster sugar

350g (12oz) jarred chestnuts in syrup

runny honey, ideally chestnut honey, to serve

In November, our chestnuts are ready for gathering. Nowadays we get our help through Helpx.net, which helps young people to travel and work in exchange for board and lodging. Our international helpers are usually here for the 10 days or two weeks of the harvest. They join us for dinner every evening and we have a simple lunch out in the courtyard in the early afternoon.

The ancient trees are planted on steep hillsides and the *cuadrilla* (team) of pickers move in a line, starting at the bottom of the hill and working upwards, as this helps with the back-breaking job. Pickers use olive branch baskets and wear rubber gloves in order to avoid the sharp spikes of the chestnut husks.

The nuts go into 50kg (110lb) sacks and are sent off to the cooperative outside Galaroza, 6km away. There they are weighed, graded, sterilised in a steam tunnel and polished before being sent off to markets around the world.

Everyone is happy once the harvest is over. In the old days when we first came here, we would light a bonfire on the last day and roast chorizo and chestnuts in the embers, to be eaten hot between slices of bread and washed down with new *mosto* (fermented grape must). Sometimes faces were painted with soot from the blackened chestnuts and, if there was enough *mosto*, there might be some singing and dancing.

Nowadays, if it's a clear starry night and the ground is damp from recent rain, we celebrate by gathering around a bonfire, roasting chestnuts in the embers, and drinking a glass or two of dry oloroso, or white wine from Huelva mulled with cinnamon, lemon juice and zest and sugar.

Slice the vanilla pod lengthways and place in a pan with the milk or cream over a low heat. When the milk begins to bubble, remove from the heat and set in a warm place for 30 minutes while the vanilla infuses. Remove the vanilla pod with a slotted spoon (dry it and put it into a jar of sugar, and in a few days you will have vanilla sugar).

Whisk the egg yolks in a heatproof bowl with the sugar and add the hot milk, stirring constantly (do not whisk vigorously or it will become foamy and will be hard to tell if the custard has thickened).

❋ Set the bowl over a saucepan of just-simmering water and stir constantly with a wooden spoon, until it is thick enough to coat the back of the spoon. Allow to cool for a few hours, then chill.

❋ Place the custard and the chestnuts with their syrup into an ice-cream machine and churn according to the manufacturer's instructions. (It might be best not to attempt this manually; it would be a little tricky with the chunks of nut.)

❋ The ice cream can be served with warmed dark chestnut honey if you have it, though other honeys are almost as good here. Spoon the ice cream into bowls, decorate with a Hazelnut tuile (see below) and enjoy with a glass of dark, syrupy Pedro Ximenez.

Hazelnut tuiles

Makes about 24

115g (4oz) hazelnuts, skins on

2 egg whites

100g (3½oz) caster sugar

1 tbsp plain flour

1 tbsp sunflower oil (or, even better, roasted hazelnut oil, if you can get it)

❋ Preheat the oven to 190ºC/375ºF/gas mark 5. Roast the hazelnuts in the oven for about 10 minutes, or until browned. Watch them carefully, as they can scorch. Transfer the hot nuts to a clean tea towel and rub them together to remove the skins. Let the nuts cool completely, then grind them finely in a food processor.

❋ Beat the egg whites until frothy. Stir in the sugar, flour, oil and the ground hazelnuts.

❋ Line two baking sheets with non-stick baking parchment or silicone sheets. Scoop rounded teaspoons of the batter on to the sheets, spacing them 10cm (4in) apart as they will spread. Using a spatula, spread the batter into very thin 7.5cm (3in) rounds.

❋ Bake the tuiles for about four minutes, or until browned around the edges. While still hot, use a metal spatula to lift them from the baking parchment and gently drape them over a rolling pin to give them their traditional curved shape. If you prefer them straight, let them cool and harden on the baking sheet instead. Either way, stick one into the top of each helping of chestnut ice cream and hand around extra on a plate. You will find the others are absent-mindedly demolished by your guests.

Helado de azafrán
Saffron ice cream

Serves 6–8

good pinch of saffron strands

175g (6oz) caster sugar

600ml (1 pint) whole milk or single cream

4 free-range egg yolks

a little runny honey, to serve

Saffron, made from the dried stigma of a crocus, is one of the most expensive spices due to the laborious and back-breaking harvesting process. The flowers grow on very short stems and each only yields a few strands. In Spain, saffron crocuses are grown on the plains of Murcia, just south of Valencia and north of Andalusia.

✳ Grind the saffron strands in a mortar with 30g (1oz) of the sugar until reduced to a powder. Place in a pan with the milk or cream over a low heat.

✳ When the milk begins to bubble, remove it from the heat and set in a warm place for 30 minutes while the saffron infuses.

✳ Cream the egg yolks briefly in a heatproof bowl with the remaining sugar and add the hot milk or cream, stirring constantly (do not whisk vigorously or it will become too foamy and will be hard to tell if the custard has thickened or not).

❋ Place the bowl over a saucepan of just-simmering water and stir continuously with a wooden spoon until it coats the back of the spoon. Allow the custard to cool for a few hours, then chill.

❋ Pour the cold custard into an ice-cream machine and churn according to the manufacturer's instructions. This can also be frozen in a shallow container in the freezer for 12 hours, but remember to beat it every three hours to stop ice crystals forming.

❋ Heat a little honey gently and pour it over the ice cream to serve.

Sorbete al romero con miel de flores de romero
Rosemary sorbet with rosemary honey

Serves 8

1 sprig of rosemary, plus sprig tops to serve

500g (1lb 2oz) granulated or caster sugar

juice of ½ lemon

½ egg white

rosemary honey, to serve

We first tasted this delicate herbal ice in Barcelona. Jeannie was determined to replicate it at home, since our hills are covered in wild rosemary. Our friend María José keeps her hives on the hills around Aracena and one of her specialities is rosemary honey, which we use in this recipe.

❋ Heat 750ml (1 pint 5fl oz) of water to boiling with the sprig of rosemary. Remove from the heat and allow to stand for 30 minutes to infuse. Don't leave it much longer, or it will become bitter and lose its fresh flavour. After 30 minutes or so, if you judge the water tastes sufficiently of rosemary, remove the sprig. Make sure you also remove all the rosemary leaves. If not, strain the liquid.

❋ Pour the rosemary-infused water into a pan with the sugar and place over a low heat to dissolve the sugar. Allow to cool.

❋ Add the lemon juice to the syrup. Tip into an ice-cream machine with the egg white and churn according to the manufacturer's instructions. In 30–40 minutes you will have a delicious sorbet.

❋ Serve straight from the machine and pour warmed rosemary honey over it. Serve with a sprig top of rosemary.

Crema de limón
Lemon cream

Serves 8–9

finely grated zest of 2 unwaxed lemons, plus the juice of 4

175g (6oz) granulated or caster sugar, plus more for the tops

6 free-range eggs

350ml (12fl oz) double cream

In winter, unwaxed fresh lemons are plentiful and cheap in our markets, so it's the perfect time to make lemon curd and lemon puddings such as this.

❋ Preheat the oven to 180ºC/350ºF/gas mark 4.

❋ Zest the two lemons into a bowl and set aside.

❋ Combine the lemon juice and sugar in a small saucepan and place over a medium-low heat to dissolve the sugar. Pour the lemon syrup over the eggs in a bowl and whisk.

❋ Bring the cream to the boil, then remove from the heat and whisk into the lemon and egg mixture.

❋ Strain the mixture through a fine sieve on to the lemon zest in its bowl and skim off any froth on the surface.

❋ Divide the lemon cream between nine 120ml (4fl oz) ovenproof dishes. (I say nine because this mixture should give you a little more than eight dishes will hold.) Try and find dishes that have a wide surface area, to give the maximum area of sugary crisp crust later.

❋ Place the dishes in a deep roasting tin. Pour boiling water from a kettle into the tin, being sure not to splash it into the dishes; it should come halfway up the sides of the dishes. Carefully place into the oven and cook for about 20 minutes, or until set.

❋ Remove from the oven and cool, then chill in the refrigerator.

❋ Remove from the fridge about 30 minutes before you want to eat and dust each with more sugar. Caramelise the sugar quickly with a blow torch. If you are having trouble with the sugar melting, sometimes a few tiny drops of water flicked on to the surface from a wet finger is enough to help. The tops should be hard and glassy.

Flan de naranja
Orange crème caramel

Serves 6–8

250g (9oz) caster sugar

juice and finely grated zest of 3 large oranges (about 200ml/7fl oz of juice)

7 large free-range egg yolks, plus 1 large whole egg

This is a different and refreshing take on the ubiquitous flan, or crème caramel, found all over Spain. This recipe comes from Valencia, which is famous for its citrus fruit.

❋ Preheat the oven to 160ºC/325ºF/gas mark 3 and arrange six 100ml (3½fl oz) dariole moulds, or ramekins, in a small, deep roasting tin. Put 50g (1¾oz) of the sugar in a small saucepan with 1 tbsp of water and heat gently for the caramel, letting it dissolve without stirring. Let it boil until it turns light brown, then remove immediately from the heat. Quickly pour a little into each mould, turning it so the caramel covers the base.

❋ Grate the orange zest on a fine zester or grater, using a little of the remaining sugar to mop up the shreds and orange oil.

❋ Beat the yolks and whole egg in a bowl very lightly with a wooden spoon, just to combine, not to make a froth.

❋ Bring the orange juice and remaining sugar to the boil, stirring to dissolve the sugar, then reduce the heat and boil for two minutes. Pour the hot juice on to the egg mixture, stirring constantly, then strain it through a sieve.

❋ Divide the mixture between the moulds. Pour boiling water from a kettle into the roasting tin to come about two-thirds of the way up the moulds, then carefully transfer the tin to the oven.

❋ Bake for 30 minutes. Remove from the oven and leave in the water until cool enough to handle; the custard will go on cooking as it cools. Remove from the water and cool on a wire rack, then chill the moulds.

❋ To serve, turn the puddings out; they will have a little pool of the caramel around them. We like to serve these with Orange and semolina fork biscuits (see right)

Crema Mora
Moorish custard cream

Serves 8

250g (9oz) root ginger, sliced

900ml (1½ pints) double cream

125g (4½oz) granulated or caster sugar

a few strands of saffron

6 free-range egg yolks, lightly beaten

A variation on the egg custard theme so often encountered in Spain. Try it with rosemary-flavoured shortbread (see page 173).

❋ Preheat the oven to 140ºC/275ºF/gas mark 1. Bring a pan of water to the boil, add the ginger and boil for 30 seconds, then drain. This takes away most of the peppery heat.

❋ Tip the cream and sugar in a pan and heat until the sugar has dissolved. When it is just below boiling point, add the ginger and saffron, turn off the heat, cover and leave to infuse for one hour.

❋ Put the yolks in a bowl. Strain the ginger and saffron cream through a sieve on to the yolks and mix well, then strain again into a jug (this eliminates any last strands of egg).

❋ Place eight 120ml (4fl oz) wide, shallow ovenproof dishes in a deep roasting tin. Pour the mixture into them, then pour enough boiling water from a kettle into the tin to come halfway up the ramekins. Carefully transfer to the oven and bake for 40 minutes until just set; they should still wobble in the middle. Remove from the tin and cool on a wire rack. When cold, chill and serve.

Orange and semolina fork biscuits

Makes 20–24

170g (6oz) unsalted butter, cut into cubes, plus more for the baking sheet

80g (2¾oz) caster sugar

30g (1oz) semolina

finely grated zest of 2 oranges

170g (6oz) plain flour

❋ Preheat the oven to 180ºC/350ºF/gas mark 4. Cream the butter and the sugar in a food processor, then gradually beat in the semolina. Grate the orange zest into the mixing bowl, pulse-blend, then add the flour and process to a soft dough. You should be able to handle the mixture straight out of the bowl (with the blade removed!). If it's too soft to handle, chill it for 20 minutes.

❋ Take pieces the size of a small walnut, roll into balls and place on a buttered baking sheet. Press them into flattish biscuits with a fork, dipped in water so as not to stick. There should be clearly defined ridges. Keep each biscuit well apart from its neighbour as they spread when cooking. Bake in the oven for 15–20 minutes.

Crema de cardamomo
Cardamom pannacotta

Serves 6

1½ x 11g (0.4oz) sachets of powdered gelatine

425ml (15fl oz) whipping cream

90g (3oz) caster sugar

1 tsp freshly ground cardamom seeds

425ml (15fl oz) Greek yogurt

fruit coulis, to serve (strawberry, raspberry, blackcurrant or quince, see Cook's note below)

mint or pineapple sage leaves, or cracked cardamom pods, to serve

A refreshing alternative to the traditional Spanish puddings based on eggs and sugar. The Spaniards have taken to yogurt in a big way in the last 25 years. The greatest acceleration came after the country joined the EU in 1985 and supermarkets are now filled with dozens of variants on the theme of yogurt- and milk-based puddings. As a change from cardamom, this pannacotta can be flavoured with lavender or saffron, anise or ginger, or rose geranium leaves.

❊ Place the gelatine in a cup with 3 tbsp of the cream and leave to soak for 10 minutes.

❊ Meanwhile place the rest of the cream in a saucepan with the sugar and cardamom and heat gently until the sugar has dissolved.

❊ Add the soaked gelatine to the warm cream and whisk over a low heat for a few seconds until well combined. Take off the heat.

❊ Stir the yogurt in a mixing bowl, then strain in the warm cream mixture through a sieve. Mix thoroughly and pour into six 150ml (5fl oz) ramekins or dariole moulds.

❊ Chill for four to six hours, until softly set. Dip the base of each mould in warm water and roll it around between your fingers; the pannacotta should just pop out.

❊ To serve, turn out on to a plate and pour fruit coulis to one side. Decorate with the herb leaves, or cracked cardamom pods.

Cook's note

TO MAKE A QUINCE COULIS *dilute a little Quince cheese (see page 210) in hot water and spoon it around the plate.*

TO MAKE SOFT FRUIT COULIS *place the fruit in a bowl with just under the same weight of caster sugar and leave to macerate for 30 minutes. Tip it into a food processor, process, then push through a nylon sieve to remove the seeds. Test for sweetness, adding more sugar if required, or lemon juice if you find it too sweet. Chill until ready to serve. We vary the fruit according to the season.*

Rosemary and chocolate creams

Serves 6–12, depending on portion size

250ml (9fl oz) white wine (we use a light Huelva wine, or a dry oloroso sherry from Gonzalez Byass for a stronger flavour)

250g (9oz) granulated or caster sugar

juice of ½ lemon

1 sprig of rosemary, plus 6 small sprig tops to serve

600ml (1 pint) double cream

150g (5½oz) best-quality dark (70% cocoa solids) chocolate, grated

4 blanched almonds, finely chopped (optional)

Rosemary and chocolate sounds an odd sort of combination, but the herbal aroma is brought to its full potential in this recipe, and the combination with the chocolate and the acid lemon is superb.

Rosemary is used often in desserts in Spain as it grows freely on the hillsides. Another of our favourites is Rosemary sorbet with rosemary honey (see page 165), or a rosemary-infused crème caramel or flan. Rosemary-flavoured shortbread is delicious, too. To make it, grind 1 tsp of rosemary needles in a coffee grinder (clean it very well afterwards, as the oil can corrode). Add it to a shortbread recipe at the same time as the flour.

❋ Pour the wine into a heavy-based pan and add the sugar, lemon juice and sprig of rosemary. Stir over a medium heat until the sugar has dissolved completely. Remove all the rosemary from the pan (strain through a sieve if necessary), then stir in the cream. Cook over a gentle heat, stirring constantly until the mixture thickens. Add the chocolate, stirring until completely melted.

❋ Bring to the boil, then reduce the heat and simmer gently for about 20 minutes, until the mixture is dark and thick, stirring often. Cool until tepid.

❋ Pour into six ceramic coffee cups or 12 espresso cups. Cover with cling film and refrigerate until set.

❋ Decorate each cup with a sprig top of rosemary and a sprinkling of chopped blanched almonds, if you like.

Tarta de peras y almendras
Pear and almond tart

Serves 10–12

For the sweet pastry

350g (12oz) plain flour

pinch of salt

175g (6oz) unsalted cold butter, cut into cubes

115g (4oz) icing sugar

3 free-range egg yolks

For the filling

6 ripe pears, peeled, cored and quartered, or same amount of Pears in syrup (see page 200)

350g (12oz) unsalted butter, softened

350g (12oz) caster sugar

350g (12oz) blanched almonds

3 free-range eggs

We always have a mass of imperfect organic pears in the orchard and, after making perry – bottling it up into cava bottles and wiring in the corks – we are still left with a mass of fruit. This frangipane tart is a great way to start to use up all that fruit, and is equally delicious with damsons or plums, peaches or apricots. We cut out the imperfections and bottle some of them in glass fruit juice jars with sugar and cinnamon (see page 200). The jars are then sterilised, so the fruit keeps all year. Damaged fruit is left on the ground and will be eaten by the sheep or the pigs.

For the sweet pastry, pulse-blend the flour, salt and butter in a food processor until it resembles breadcrumbs. Add the icing sugar and egg yolks and pulse again. The pastry will combine and leave the edges of the bowl. Wrap in cling film and chill for one hour.

Preheat the oven to 180ºC/350ºF/gas mark 4.

Coarsely grate the chilled pastry into a 30cm (12in) loose-based flan tin, then press it evenly over the base and up the sides. Line the tin with greaseproof paper, fill with baking beans and bake for 20 minutes until light brown. Remove the paper and beans and leave to cool.

Place the pear quarters in the pastry case, narrow ends pointing into the centre; that way they will fit together. If using bottled or canned fruit, make sure it is well drained before you put it into the pastry case, to avoid a soggy bottom.

Preheat the oven to 150ºC/300ºF/gas mark 3.

For the filling, cream the butter and sugar until pale and light. Put the almonds in a food processor and chop until fine. Add the butter and sugar and blend, then beat in the eggs one by one. Pour the mixture over the pears and bake for 40 minutes.

Serve with a little cold pouring cream.

Tarta Beatriz
Beatrice's gateau

Serves 12

4 large oranges, washed

1 thin-skinned unwaxed lemon, washed

unsalted butter, for the tin

plain flour, for the tin

10 free-range eggs

500g (1lb 2oz) blanched almonds

500g (1lb 2oz) granulated or caster sugar

2 tsp baking powder

This cake is probably Spanish in origin, but it has emigrated to Australia and back. There are many variations on almond and citrus cakes all through the Mediterranean world. However, we were in fact given this recipe by a friend from Sydney... who we met when he was organising the Vatican Pavilion at Expo '92 in Seville.

Our friend's alter ego, Beatrice, is almost certainly the personal friend of Priscilla, queen of the desert, and this cake was presented to us as 'Gâteau Beatrice'. The chocolate ganache should go on as thick as Bea's pan stick make-up.

You can serve the cakes plain with or without a little cream, or make an orange buttercream for the centre and place one on top of the other, or fill with apricot jam puréed with lemon juice.

To go eastern Med, you can sprinkle the cake with honey and orange flower water, adding an inauthentic but delicious splash of Grand Marnier or Cointreau.

If you are going whole hog for Bea's version, then apricot jam filling and Chocolate ganache covering (see right) is the answer. Halfway between Vienna and Beirut!

❊ Put the oranges and lemon in a pressure cooker with 500ml (18fl oz) of water and cook for 15–20 minutes until soft, or cook them in boiling water in a covered pan on the stove for 40 minutes. Spoon them out and allow to cool on a deep plate.

❊ Preheat the oven to 200ºC/400ºF/gas mark 6. Butter two 20cm (8in) cake tins, ideally with removable bases. Dust with flour, then roll the tins around, tapping, until coated. Tip out the excess.

❊ Beat the eggs in a bowl until whites and yolks are well amalgamated.

❊ Grind three-quarters of the almonds in a food processor, then throw in the last one-quarter and grind only for a short while, so they remain only coarsely chopped.

❊ Now mix the sugar, fresh-ground almonds and baking powder in a large bowl.

❋ Transfer the tepid oranges and lemon into the food processor and purée the fruits, skins and all. It is OK to leave one or two coarser bits of skin. Tip the beaten eggs and the orange mixture over the dry ingredients and stir well.

❋ Now pour into the prepared tins and bake for about one hour.

❋ Have a look at the cake and, if it is still sloppy-looking in the centre, cook it for another five minutes or so. Try not to burn the top (if it is getting dark, greaseproof paper laid over is a good idea). Test the cake by inserting a skewer; it should emerge clean. When it does, remove from the oven and allow to cool before turning out.

Chocolate ganache

Enough to cover a 20cm (8in) cake

150g (5½oz) best-quality dark (70% cocoa solids) chocolate, broken into pieces

150ml (5fl oz) double cream

Don't try to speed up any part of the process by putting this in the refrigerator, or else the glossy shine of the chocolate will be lost.

❋ Melt the chocolate and cream together, stirring constantly. Remove from the heat, cover and allow the ganache to reach room temperature, checking for consistency from time to time.

❋ When it is thick, but before it solidifies (after about two and a half hours), pour the ganache over the cake. After four hours it should have set.

Tarta de miel y cítricos
Citrus and honey cake

Serves 12

For the cake

175g (6oz) unsalted butter, softened, plus more for the tin

plain flour, for the tin

1 orange, washed

1 thin-skinned unwaxed lemon, washed

25g (scant 1oz) roasted hazelnuts, plus 12 whole hazelnuts to decorate (optional)

115g (4oz) almonds

175g (6oz) demerara sugar

3 large free-range eggs

250g (9oz) semolina

1 tsp baking powder

For the sauce

225ml (8fl oz) runny honey, ideally orange blossom honey

4cm (1½in) cinnamon stick

juice of 1 orange

juice of ½ lemon

crème fraîche, or a mixture of whipped cream with yogurt, to serve (optional)

One of the joys of running a guest house is that we meet people from all over the world and, inevitably, as we sit around the dining table, the conversation turns to food. In 1992, while the Expo in Seville was going on, several delegates from the Turkish pavilion came up to stay one weekend, and we talked about Turkish food and the food of the Eastern Mediterranean. Several years later we were happy to receive a book of hazelnut recipes sent to us by the Turkish hazelnut promotion board. This is an eastern Mediterranean cake which is perfectly in tune with Spanish ingredients.

✻Preheat the oven to 200ºC/400ºF/gas mark 6. Butter a 25cm (10in) springform cake tin and line the base with greaseproof paper. Butter the paper too, then dust with plain flour, turning to coat the tin and tapping out the excess.

✻Cut the orange and lemon into quarters and remove all the pips.

✻Grind up the nuts in a food processor, then add the citrus fruit and process together. It's good to leave some of the nuts slightly coarse, as it lends texture to the cake, and it's also not bad to encounter the odd bit of roughly chopped peel, so don't worry if it is not entirely smooth.

✻Beat together the butter, sugar, eggs, semolina and baking powder until you have a smooth mix. Stir in the fruit and nut purée.

✻Spoon the mixture into the prepared tin, place on a central oven shelf and bake for 10 minutes. Reduce the oven temperature to 180ºC/350ºF/gas mark 4 and bake for a further 45 minutes.

✻Remove the cake and cool for five minutes. If you have buttered and floured your tin properly, it should come away easily from the sides when you unclip them. Remove the papers and place the cake on a wire rack over a wide plate.

✻Make a flavoured syrup by simmering the honey with 5 tbsp of water and the cinnamon stick for five minutes. Fish out the cinnamon stick and add the citrus juices.

cont...

Prick the cake all over and pour the syrup on to it, distributing it as widely as possible, as you want the whole cake to be dampened. Any juice which goes straight through on to the plate can be spooned back over when the cake is cold and on its serving dish.

Have ready in a bowl some crème fraîche, or a mixture of whipped cream and yogurt and, just before serving, spread a thin layer on top of the cake and decorate with the roasted hazelnuts, split in half, if you like. Cut the cake at the table and hand around the rest of the cream in a bowl with a small spoon or sauce ladle.

Ginger roulade

Serves 8–10

85g (3oz) unsalted butter

225g (8oz) golden syrup or treacle

60g (2oz) granulated or caster sugar

115g (4oz) plain flour

1 tsp baking powder

1 tsp ground ginger

1 tsp ground cinnamon

1 tsp ground allspice

1 tsp ground nutmeg

1 free-range egg, separated

500ml (18fl oz) whipping cream, whipped

a few marrons glacés, chopped, or finely chopped stem ginger (optional)

icing sugar, to serve

This recipe was given to me by my sister Bumble, who lives in Scotland. It's perfect for autumn and can be served with chopped marrons glacés in the cream filling. We usually buy them ready made from Galicia as the physical structure of our own chestnuts, with their ridges and indentations, make them unsuitable for candying. If you use treacle you will get a darker, saltier flavoured roulade with the faint liquorice flavour molasses brings with it. If you prefer a lighter ginger sponge, then go for golden syrup.

Preheat the oven to 180ºC/350ºF/gas mark 4.

In a heavy-based saucepan over a medium heat, melt the butter, syrup or treacle and sugar with 115ml (4fl oz) of water.

Mix the flour with the baking powder and spices and, when the liquids have melted and cooled, add the dry ingredients to them with the egg yolk. Beat the egg white until it forms stiff peaks, then fold into the mixture.

Line a Swiss roll tin with greaseproof paper or a silicone sheet, pour in the mixture and bake in the oven for 12–15 minutes.

Cover with a damp tea towel and allow to cool.

Turn the sponge out of the tin and remove the papers. Mix the whipped cream with the marrons glacés or, for a more intense ginger flavour, the stem ginger, or neither, spread it over the cake, then roll it up. Sift over icing sugar to serve.

Tarta de almendras y chocolate
Chocolate and almond cake

Serves 8–12

For the cake

115g (4oz) unsalted butter, plus more for the tin

plain flour, for the tin

115g (4oz) best-quality dark (70% cocoa solids) chocolate

2 tbsp Spanish brandy

50g (1¾oz) blanched almonds

115g (4oz) granulated or caster sugar, plus 1 tbsp

3 free-range eggs, separated

For the icing

115g (4oz) best-quality dark (70% cocoa solids) chocolate

55g (2oz) icing sugar

2 tbsp Spanish brandy

115g (4oz) unsalted butter

icing sugar, to dust

This moist, rich chocolate cake is made with whole almonds and, like many of the cakes we bake at Buenvino, it uses no flour.

❋ Preheat the oven to 180ºC/350ºF/gas mark 4.

❋ Line the bases of two 20cm (8in) cake tins with greaseproof or silicone paper. Brush the bases and sides with butter and dust with a little flour, turning to coat the tin and tapping out the excess.

❋ Melt the chocolate with the brandy in a heatproof bowl over barely simmering water. Let cool. Grind the almonds in a food processor; they should be left a little gritty, not ground to a paste.

❋ In a separate bowl, cream the butter and the 115g (4oz) of sugar, beating until light and fluffy. Beat in the egg yolks one by one.

❋ In a third bowl, beat the egg whites until stiff, then add the 1 tbsp of sugar and continue whisking until stiff peaks form. Add the melted, cooled chocolate to the butter mixture with half the ground almonds. Fold in half the egg whites, followed by the remaining almonds; then the remaining egg white.

❋ Divide the mixture between the prepared tins and make a dip in the centre of each cake. Bake in the oven for 20–25 minutes. The cake should be moist and slightly unset at the centre.

❋ Allow to cool for a few minutes, then turn out on to a wire rack, remove the papers and allow to get cold.

❋ For the icing, melt the chocolate, icing sugar and brandy in a heatproof bowl over simmering water, then whisk in the butter bit by bit. Remove from the heat and whisk occasionally until cool.

❋ When the cake is cold, fill and ice it with the chocolate icing. Dust with icing sugar. Delicious with a chilled glass of Croft Original pale cream sherry.

In my storecupboard

From top: turmeric; chilli flakes;
dried oregano; za'atar; pimientón
de la vera; sea salt

The kitchen storecupboard is the backbone of any
cook's arrangements, especially if he or she lives in
the country and far from the shops. It is even more
critical if ingredients are not available in the local market
town. When we first lived at Finca Buenvino we found it
difficult to buy butter or cream, for example, which were not
part of the local culture. We used to drive 60km to Portugal to
find butter in the first small village over the border.

Olive oil was plentiful and local, but it was roughly
made in the old village cooperatives in those days; slightly
bitter with high acidity. Children had it on bread for their
afternoon snack, sprinkled with a little sugar, or it was taken
on toast in the bars for breakfast; a healthy alternative to
rendered pork fat with smoked paprika.

Nowadays, most of the very local olive cooperatives have closed down; the tiny olive groves dotted about the highest part of our natural park are no longer commercially viable and many have been abandoned and are overgrown by brambles. The Code Napoléon has meant that small estates have been divided up into yet smaller patches upon inheritance. After several generations, a family might be left with five trees on the top of a precipitous hillside. Whereas the old men of the last generation were happy to ride out on a donkey (with a terrier standing up on the donkey's neck, to keep its owner company!) to prune the trees, clean up the brambles or pick the fruit, the young people of today have been educated for a different, more urban lifestyle. A mortgage, a car on the HP and a job as a mechanic might be the way to go, and five inaccessible olive trees are never going to produce an income. The idea of having to climb a steep hill and collect the olives with mules or donkeys can only appeal to the romantic.

Not far away however, at a lower altitude, excellent oil is produced from the more extensive groves of Santa Olalla and Zufre. Further afield still, in the flat lands around Beas, award-winning extra virgin olive oil is pressed, and in the mountains of Seville, where land holdings are larger, in Guadalcanal and Cazalla de la Sierra, excellent oil is made. East of Seville are the vast olive landscapes of Jaén and Córdoba, whence come delicious varietal oils.

In my store you will find several large (five-litre) containers of olive oil. It is probably the most important ingredient in my day-to-day cooking. I always have two kinds of olive oil. Virgin cold-pressed arbequina is for dressing green or tomato salads, for making a mustardy vinaigrette to dress warm cooked potatoes to be eaten with fresh herbs and raw sweet onion, or for putting on toast for breakfast. I also use it for making Andalusian scrambled eggs: for every two eggs, fill half an eggshell with arbequina oil and tip it over the eggs in a high-sided non-stick saucepan. Add a pinch of salt. Now beat vigorously with a non-stick heatproof silicone spatula. When the oil and the eggs are blended, put the pan over a high gas flame and keep stirring gently, easing the eggs from the sides and the base of the pan. Remove from the heat while some of the egg is still a little runny and tip on to a slice of toast. No butter, healthy and delicious.

The other olive oil I use comes from a second pressing; it's paler in colour and lighter in flavour, perfect for garlic mayonnaise to serve with cold boiled prawns. I also use it for gently cooking potatoes for a Spanish tortilla, or for softening onions or garlic. Really, olive oil should only be used for quietly 'braising' rather than for frying anything to a crisp at high heat, which affects its flavour.

I would use sunflower oil if I wanted to make potato chips with whole garlic cloves in their skins, for instance. When the chips are golden, tip them on to kitchen paper to dry, remove the garlic cloves with tongs and allow them to cool while the potatoes are kept warm in the oven. When they are cool enough to handle, squeeze the garlic

cloves until the soft centres protrude. There will be some parts which are toasted or singed, but these only add to the flavour. Drop the garlic 'innards' on to the potatoes before taking them to the table. (In our part of Spain, they are often served with paper-thin slices of melting jamón on top, or an egg fried in olive oil.)

Herbs and spices

Aniseed

Similar in flavour to star anise, but less overpowering, we use these in the preparation of our salchichón.

Black pepper

A staple; peppercorns to grind or drop whole into stews, or to add as a seasoning with salt to most savoury dishes.

Cardamom pods (green)

We use these in pannacotta (see page 170) and also in rice pilaf. The pods can also be used when making a syrup for fruits, or in Tomato and cardamom jam (see page 208).

Cinnamon sticks

For flavouring tagines and stews. Also to sprinkle on Moroccan tomato and almond salad (see page 143).

Cloves

We use these in game and fowl dishes, sometimes ground into a picada with cloves, chocolate and almonds to add to a venison, hare, or even beef casserole. Anchovies and cloves are vital to a good pissaladière. We also put cloves in our pickled cherries and plums and into our morcilla and salchichón.

Cumin

These seeds, lightly toasted in a dry pan and ground in a mortar, are essential in local *cocidos* or Moroccan tagines.

Fennel seeds

Subtly different to aniseed and yet reminiscent of them. We use them to make our *finocchio* sausages.

Flor de sal

Soft sea salt from the pans of Cádiz, or from Olhão in Portugal. This is ideal for sprinkling on fried peppers and garlic. We also keep coarse sea salt from Cádiz (*sal marina*), that we use for cooking and for baking *dorada* or *lubina a la sal* (whole sea bass or bream cooked in a crust of salt, see page 89).

Ginger (root)

Although this does not strictly live in the storecupboard, we always have it to hand in the freezer, where it keeps wonderfully. It can be sliced to add to tagines, or grated for baking or for infusions.

Lavender

Every year we collect the flowers and use them for cooking, making lavender ice creams or pannacottas.

Nutmeg

Sometimes we use this, grated, on crema catalana instead of cinnamon. It is also good in spinach and chard dishes and it improves chicken stock and potato-thickened winter soups.

Oregano, dried

We pick this in the woods below the house, where it grows wild. It's essential on freshly picked beef tomatoes, sprinkled with sea salt; one of the simplest summer tapas (see page 44). We also infuse it into a syrup which is excellent with fruit (see page 157).

Pimientón de la vera

Both kinds of this smoked paprika, hot and sweet, come from the southern foothills of the Gredos mountains, south west of Madrid. La Vera is an area of great natural beauty; there are forests and, lower down, the fields where the peppers are grown, along with fields of tobacco. Pimientón de la Vera is always smoked, as the peppers ripen just when the autumn rains are likely to appear and they therefore cannot be dried in the sun. The traditional drying building has smouldering oak braziers on the ground floor and the peppers are spread out on an upper slatted wooden floor. The roof has vents to let the smoke out. Both varieties of paprika are packaged in similar tins (see the photo on page 199). Look out for the word *picante* on hot pepper, or *dulce* on sweet pepper.

Saffron

From Murcia, Valencia or Tarragona. The scarlet stamens of the saffron crocus provide a musky flavour and glorious celebratory yellow colour in paellas and pilafs, or in our favourite golden ice cream in which saffron marries happily with honey (see page 164).

Smoked salt

Gives a smoky flavour to barbecued fish or chicken.

Star anise

Powerfully scented, we keep a small quantity of this for use when making anise syrups for flavouring, and in our pisto (see page 149).

Thyme, dried

This is no substitute for the fresh herb, but it is useful if you have nowhere to grow thyme in a pot.

Turmeric

Not European at all, this rhizome came into Maghrebi use via Persia. We use it in our Romería chicken (see page 113) for a glorious golden colour, and in an unusual local dish of potatoes, almonds and salt cod, *Papas en amarillo con bacalao* (see page 103).

Vanilla pods

For ice creams, pannacottas and custards.

Nuts, seeds, pulses and fruits

Almonds

We use blanched almonds for cold Ajo blanco and also for making praline to decorate our Seville orange soufflé (see pages 72 and 155). We fry them in olive oil and serve them sprinkled with salt and sometimes spices (see page 44), to eat with a glass of sherry. Raw almonds in their skins can be dipped into half a lightly beaten egg white mixed with a tiny bit of water, then rolled in a mixture of sea salt and cinnamon and baked on a shallow tray in the oven.

THE BUENVINO COOKBOOK

Chickpeas

We prefer the *Blanco Lechoso* variety, also known as Andalusian. Soak them overnight in plenty of water, with a spoonful of bicarbonate of soda. By morning they will have swollen. When cooked they retain a nutty texture and flavour, which bears no resemblance to the fudge-like texture of bottled chickpeas. However, I do keep some bottled chickpeas as well, as they are a tremendous time saver if there is a sudden influx and I need to make a selection of tapas.

Dried fruit

We keep a pot each of dried figs and dried apricots. Useful for winter compotes, or for chopping and adding to our home-made granola, or for some tagines.

Hazelnuts, roasted

Important in picadas, such as for a Catalan *suquet* of fish or quails.

Pine nuts

We use these in baking, and sometimes in our pestos. We also fry them lightly in a dry pan and toss them into salads.

Pistachios, shelled and roasted

We get these freshly toasted from E & A Gispert behind Santa María del Mar in Barcelona. They are spectacular in some meat dishes, or sprinkled over oranges in syrup.

Seeds, other

Pumpkin seeds, linseeds and sunflower seeds are useful to have on hand; all go into salads and bread loaves.

Sesame seeds, toasted

A vital ingredient of Middle Eastern za'atar, make your own by mixing the seeds with dried thyme and salt flakes and pack it into a tightly lidded jar. Sesame seeds are also delicious in wholemeal loaves and in pastries.

Walnuts

For use in picadas or some salads.

About pulses

Pulses play a big part in our kitchen. We have lentils from Castile: small *pardinas* and larger *castellanas*. The larger are good in soups, while the smaller I serve al dente, either dressed in oil and vinegar with yogurt, garlic and spices (cinnamon, pepper, ground cardamom and plenty of chopped parsley are good) or warm with duck breast or pork fillet, with the meat juices poured over and stirred into the lentils. Place the sliced meat on top and, for colour, decorate with finely chopped parsley and strips of *pimientos del piquillo* from a jar or can.

Most of the beans we eat today in Spain originally came to us from the Americas, and were unknown here before *la conquista*. They are useful, both dried (which I prefer for beans and chickpeas, even though it involves a long soak and a long cook in boiling water) and canned or in jars, for those sudden visitor emergencies. I keep different types, and use them for their various colours and textures rather than much difference in flavour. If I am cooking Swiss chard with beans, as in Rice with snails and chard (see page 85), I like to include *morada* or *pinta* beans. The former are speckled when raw, the latter a solid purplish pink. *Canella* beans are more orangey in colour but turn brownish when cooked; they look good in a squid ink dish where you get the effect of African art colours of charcoal and brown.

The bean with the strongest flavour is the *judión* or *granja* bean, which we know as butter bean in England. It's my personal favourite, either with clams and tomato, or cooked with chorizo, pork and black pudding in my version of a typical Asturian *fabada*.

With canned beans you can improvise for an unexpected visitor, perhaps draining them, dressing them in a vinaigrette, slicing raw sweet onions into the thinnest of rings, and shredding on the flakes of yesterday's leftover grilled sardines (when cold, the flesh comes easily away from the bones), or the contents of a can of tuna. Chop coriander leaves or basil leaves over the top. I would use a can of *pinta* or *morada* beans for this. When it comes to white beans, I would drain them and dress them with chopped Sun-dried tomatoes (see page 214) from my storecupboard, with lots of finely chopped parsley leaves and perhaps a shot of chilli oil or a squeeze of tomato purée from a tube. Don't forget the onions! It's up to you to be inventive and time-saving products, honestly and well made, are not to be scorned.

Odds and ends

In southern Spain it is important to be on the alert for friends and acquaintances dropping in at any time. There is a less formal approach to visiting or entertaining than there is in northern Europe. You might not be invited to have lunch or to dine with friends, but they will not be surprised if you arrive on their doorstep, and are always pleased to see you and ready with an offer of refreshment, both food and drink depending on the hour. It is customary to refuse an offer when it is initially made but, if repeated, it would be churlish not to accept.

We always try to have jamón, salchichón, chorizo and mature manchego cheese to hand. Also canned or bottled olives in brine, stuffed with anchovies or jalapeño peppers, or flavoured with lemon. Locally pickled olives tend to be flavoured with fennel branches and bitter orange peel.

Tiny breadsticks, or *picos*, are usually served with jamón and other charcuterie.

Canned or bottled chickpeas will do if you are in a hurry to make houmous, or a hot dish of chickpeas and spinach.

Garlic and onions are always in the vegetable rack.

Canned tuna is useful for a quick delicious salad with canned, roasted *pimientos del piquillo* and toasted garlic.

Capers and caperberries in brine are also useful. Capers for tomato salads, potato salads, and tapenade. Caperberries to crunch as tapas, perhaps with a G&T rather than wine, as they are quite vinegary and would spoil a delicate white or a rosé; however oloroso, or even a light manzanilla will tolerate them, even be polite to them.

Prepared items

We also keep preparations which can be used in the making of our dishes. Here is a selection:

Aubergines

Aubergines candied in honey (see page 202)
These are great with manchego cheese or fresh goat's cheese, when we want a change from quince cheese.

Pickled aubergines (see page 196)
A useful tapas dish.

Lemons

Preserved lemons in oil and Indian-style pickled lemons (see pages 205 and 206)
We use these in our tagines or to eat with curries.

Mushrooms

Dried boletus (porcini in Italy, ceps in France, the local name here is *tentullos*). We slice the mushrooms and dry them on racks over the Rayburn cooker. Once dry, they last all year in a glass jar.

Oils

Lemon oil, Basil oil (see pages 207 and 211)
We make these infusions with a mixture of sunflower and olive oils. Olive oil alone is too strong a flavour, even the second pressing, so we cut it with almost-flavourless sunflower oil. If you are using a 1 litre (1¾ pint) jar, for instance, you would only use about 200ml (7fl oz) of olive oil.

Quince and pears

Quince cheese (see page 210)
This is the quince paste we make in the autumn. We pick the quinces in October.

Pears in syrup (see page 200)
We have orchards of pears down in the valley at Finca Buenvino. We pick the pears in September and bottle them in syrup.

Sugar

Vanilla sugar
Useful in puddings and cakes. Our used, then dried, vanilla pods go into a jar with sugar, gradually infusing it over the weeks.

Tomatoes

Bottled tomatoes (see page 213)
We bottle about 100 litres (21 gallons) of tomatoes in September and sterilise them in a bain marie. By June or July the following year we have used them all up.

Green tomato, pear and chilli chutney (see page 199)
Sam's grandmother's recipe, this is a good way to use up all the green tomatoes left over in the orchard at the end of summer. Great with cheese and cold meat.

Sun-dried tomatoes (see page 214)
We dry these and bottle them in oil during July and August, and then have a supply for the year.

Spicy tomato ketchup (see page 212)
Our own recipe, containing cloves and onions. Delicious with cold meats and an important ingredient for our Barbecued Iberian pork ribs (see page 213).

Storecupboard recipes

Here are some useful products which can be made up for the storecupboard. I've not gone in much for jams and marmalades, which we make anyway and which are fairly well known, so these recipes are perhaps more unusual for the home cook.

Berenjenas en vinagre
Pickled aubergines

Makes 2 x 1 litre (1¾ pint) jars

2kg (4lb 8oz) aubergines

salt

1.2 litres (2 pints) white wine vinegar

600ml (1 pint) red wine vinegar

3 garlic cloves, finely sliced

basil leaves, torn, or whole oregano leaves

extra virgin olive oil (just pour until the job is done!)

When we were recently married, driving south from England to Spain, we made a detour to visit friends of Sam's in Alsace Lorraine. We left their house with a magnificent red wine vinegar 'mother' (the live culture which makes vinegar from wine), and she is still with us today.

There is often red wine left over at the end of a dinner here, either in glasses or in the bottle, and it is tipped straight on to our mother. Occasionally, if she is looking parched, we feed her with a whole bottle of rioja or Ribera del Duero, either a young wine or a crianza, but if you own one of these mothers you can't feed her with trash; a corked bottle, for instance, is best thrown away.

Our cookery course guests often take a little away with them and we know that she has children in Scotland, America and Australia!

If you are feeling enthusiastic and thrifty, and don't mind the hint of aubergine, collect the vinegar after use here, bring it to the boil with a couple of bay leaves and some peppercorns, reduce it by half, add 4 tbsp of treacle, then return to a boil, stirring until the treacle and vinegar meld, to make your own balsamic vinegar.

This recipe is from the south of Italy, and was given to me by the American-Italian mother of a good friend and neighbour who lives on a remote farm. I have tweaked it a little.

Wash the aubergines, then slice them into discs about ½cm (¼in) thick. If you use a mandolin or food processor it's simpler to obtain uniform slices. If you want to have really thin strips of pickled aubergine, to wrap around salted anchovies or fresh cheese pegged with a cocktail stick, then it's best to use a potato peeler. Discard the first strips which will be nearly all skin, but the strip of skin down the side of most of the slices is not only attractive but holds them together.

🔥 If using a mixture of thick or thin slices, keep them separate, or prepare them on different days. Layer the aubergine pieces in a bowl with a sprinkling of salt. Cover with cling film and leave in a cool corner overnight. (Or refrigerate them, if you prefer.)

🔥 In the morning, pour off the accumulated juices and tip the aubergines into a colander or sieve. Run cold water over them to get rid of the salt and then press them to extract as much liquid as possible. When they are dryish, spread them on to a tea towel on the kitchen counter so they dry further, or put them out in the sunlight. Leave them for 30–40 minutes.

🔥 Meanwhile, tip the two vinegars into a non-reactive stainless steel saucepan and bring to the boil. Reduce the heat to a simmer, tip the aubergines into the vinegar and return to the boil. Cook for five minutes, but no longer; you don't want the slices to disintegrate.

🔥 Remove from the heat and strain over the sink, collecting the vinegar if you like, pressing the aubergine slices down slightly.

cont...

🌿 Put some kitchen paper on a work top. (Not a marble work top, or the vinegar will eat into it. In this case, put a board under the paper.) Spread out the aubergine pieces and allow them to dry for about two hours. As it's usually sunny here at aubergine time, I prefer to do this under the sun.

🌿 Now sterilise a couple of 1-litre (1¼-pint) Kilner jars and lids, or their equivalent. You can buy continental ring-sealed jars with clip tops or screwtops almost anywhere nowadays. To sterilise them, I preheat the oven to 110ºC/225ºF/gas mark ¼, put the jars in on their sides and cook for five to 10 minutes. (If they have rubber rings, boil those separately in water.) Alternatively, you can put the jars and lids into a tall-sided pan, cover with water, then bring to the boil and boil for 10–20 minutes. It's a good idea to pack a tea towel in with them to stop them rattling about and chipping or breaking.

🌿 When the jars are dry and cool, drop a layer of garlic slices and herbs in each jar and pour over a thin layer of extra virgin olive oil.

🌿 Now cover with a thicker layer of aubergine, a sprinkle of olive oil, then another thin layer of herbs and garlic. Sprinkle with oil and continue on up to the top of the jar. I don't think it matters which you end up with, herbs and garlic or aubergine, but do make sure you have left yourself enough of the former to flavour your second jar. If you have not got enough garlic or herbs, you will just have to prepare some more at this point.

🌿 When the jars are loosely full, pour olive oil up to the top of the jar and press down the aubergines with something which fits, perhaps a circular potato masher. You want everything to be covered in oil and the aubergines will drink it all in, as you will know only too well from frying them!

🌿 Store the jars in a cool larder. They will be ready for eating in a couple of months, but will improve over the next six months.

Green tomato, pear and chilli chutney

Makes about 4kg (9lb)

1kg (2lb 4oz) green tomatoes, chopped

finely grated zest of
1 unwaxed lemon

12 dried chillies, finely chopped, or a shot of Tabasco, or
1 tsp chilli powder

1kg (2lb 4oz) apples, peeled, cored and sliced

250g (9oz) sliced onions

500g (1lb 2oz) raisins or sultanas

2 tsp ground ginger

2 tsp grated nutmeg

2 tsp ground cinnamon

2 tsp crushed black peppercorns

2 cloves

2 tbsp salt

2 garlic cloves, finely chopped

1.2 litres (2 pints) white wine vinegar

2 large pears

750g (1lb 10oz) brown sugar

Another way of using up pears, and also the large quantity of green tomatoes which we are left with at the end of the summer. This is based on Sam's Irish grandmother's recipe.

🌿 Put all the ingredients except the vinegar, pears and sugar into a non-reactive stainless steel saucepan. Moisten with a little of the vinegar. Cook gently, adding the rest of the vinegar as the chutney boils down, for 30 minutes.

🌿 Now add the peeled, cored and chopped pears and the sugar. Return to a gentle boil as the sugar melts, then, once it has all dissolved, reduce to a simmer for another 30 minutes. Towards the end, stir constantly (as they thicken, chutneys catch very easily). When the mixture is of a jam-like consistency, it is ready.

🌿 Pour into warm sterilised jars (see opposite) and cover when cold. Keeps for years.

Pears in syrup

Makes 1kg (2lb 4oz) jar

6–8 pears

juice of 1 lemon

250g (9oz) granulated sugar

1 cinnamon stick, plus more for the jar

Use firm pears, such as Conference.

🔥 Peel the pears and cut into quarters, removing the cores. Drop the slices into a saucepan containing 500ml (18fl oz) of water acidulated with the lemon juice to stop them turning brown.

🔥 Put the granulated sugar into a separate deep pan with 100ml (3½fl oz) of water and the cinnamon stick, snapped in two. Place over a low heat until the sugar has dissolved.

🔥 Meanwhile, bring the pears to the boil in the lemony liquid in which they have been keeping. Tip in the contents of the sugar syrup pan and return to the boil, then remove from the heat.

🔥 Fish out the pears with a slotted spoon, and pack into a 1kg (2lb 4oz) sterilised Kilner jar (see page 198), poking a stick of cinnamon in, too. Pour on the syrup, seal the jar and sterilise by bringing to the boil in a bain marie, then leaving to cool in the water.

Fig caviar

Serves up to 12, spread on toasted bread

½ green pepper

125ml (4fl oz) extra virgin olive oil, plus 1 tbsp

1 sweet white or red onion, finely chopped

3 tomatoes, skinned and deseeded (see page 96)

10 black figs, peeled

salt and freshly ground black pepper

juice of 1 lemon

Not strictly to be kept in the storecupboard, this will last a week in the fridge. It can be served at tapas time, spread on to a warm slice of toasted bread and accompanied by a very cold glass of white wine.

❲ The night before you make this, place the half green pepper in a small bowl and cover with the 125ml (4fl oz) of extra virgin olive oil. Cover and leave to infuse overnight.

❲ Heat the 1 tbsp of oil in a saucepan and cook the onion, tomatoes and figs, simmering together for 25–30 minutes,

❲ Remove the green pepper from the bowl of olive oil. If you want a stronger flavour, bash it up in a mortar and strain the resulting green juice through a sieve.

❲ Allow the fig mixture to cool, then tip it into a food processor and pulse-blend gently, slowly adding the green pepper-infused oil. Place in a bowl. Season with salt, pepper and lemon juice, stirring all the while with a wooden spoon, until you have the right balance of salt and acidity. Cover and keep in the fridge until needed.

Berenjenas con miel
Aubergines candied in honey

Makes 8

8 very firm aubergines, stems left on, small enough to fit into wide-mouthed preserving jars

juice of 4 lemons

1kg (2lb 4oz) granulated sugar

1 hand root ginger, sliced

3 chillies, chopped (seeds left in)

1.2l (2 pints) honey

olive oil, to seal

You've almost certainly noticed how aubergines always drink up all the oil in the pan when you are frying them. In fact they will drink *any* liquid into which they are placed and this is what makes them perfect for candying. They can be flavoured with cloves, cardamom or anise, but we like to eat them with cheese and find that ginger and chilli give the right flavour. This is an Algerian recipe and is a great way of dealing with a glut of aubergines in the orchard.

This recipe is not as complicated as it initially looks. It takes a few days to carry out, but it's only a short time spent each day and is worth the effort. I initially made this dish because I was at my wit's end trying to find new ways of dealing with our glut of aubergines… there is only so much ratatouille or baba ghanoush that one can present to guests every week. Everybody who has tried them loves them and I'm always being told to open a factory and make them commercially! The very smallest might be good dipped in dark chocolate…

These are delicious with a good manchego or pecorino cheese. The aubergines should be whole and have their stems left on, and be served with some of their syrup. They look attractive on the plate and are immediately recognisable for what they are, even though they taste utterly different and have become completely transparent. They are also good with vanilla ice cream.

They will keep for six months or so in a cool larder.

Peel the aubergines with a potato-peeler up to the pointed clasps, which seem to anchor the fruit to its stem. Leave these intact as they look pretty when the fruit is ready. Prick them all over with a fork. Drop them immediately into a pan of cold water acidulated with the juice of one lemon. Make sure the aubergines are completely covered with the water by fitting a plate into the saucepan and putting a weight on top, such as a jam jar.

Leave to soak for 36 hours, changing the water every 12 hours and adding fresh lemon juice. The brownish water which you throw away will be removing any bitterness from the aubergines. Drain the aubergines and set aside.

Dissolve half the sugar in 1.2 litres (2 pints) of water over a medium heat and bring to the boil. Squeeze another lemon and pour the juice into the syrup. Drop in the ginger and chillies and gently slide the aubergines into the liquid with a slotted spoon without breaking them. Return to the boil, then turn off the heat. You don't want the aubergines breaking up, so just leave to cool. Cover with the plate and weight and stand for a day in a cool place.

Another 24 hours. Still going well.

Next day, remove the aubergines from the syrup with a slotted spoon, and set aside on a plate. Strengthen the sugar syrup with the rest of the sugar. Heat gently until all is dissolved, then bring to the boil. Slide the aubergines back into the syrup with the slotted spoon, return to the boil, then turn off the heat. Allow to stand for another day in a cool place, with the weighted plate over the fruit.

Another day and a night!

On the following day, remove the aubergines once more with the slotted spoon, and place them on a plate. They should be beginning to turn translucent, having absorbed a lot of sugar. Add the honey to the liquid syrup and gently bring to the boil. Carefully slide the aubergines back into the honey-thickened syrup and return to the boil. Simmer very gently for 10 minutes, or until the aubergines have become translucent.

cont...

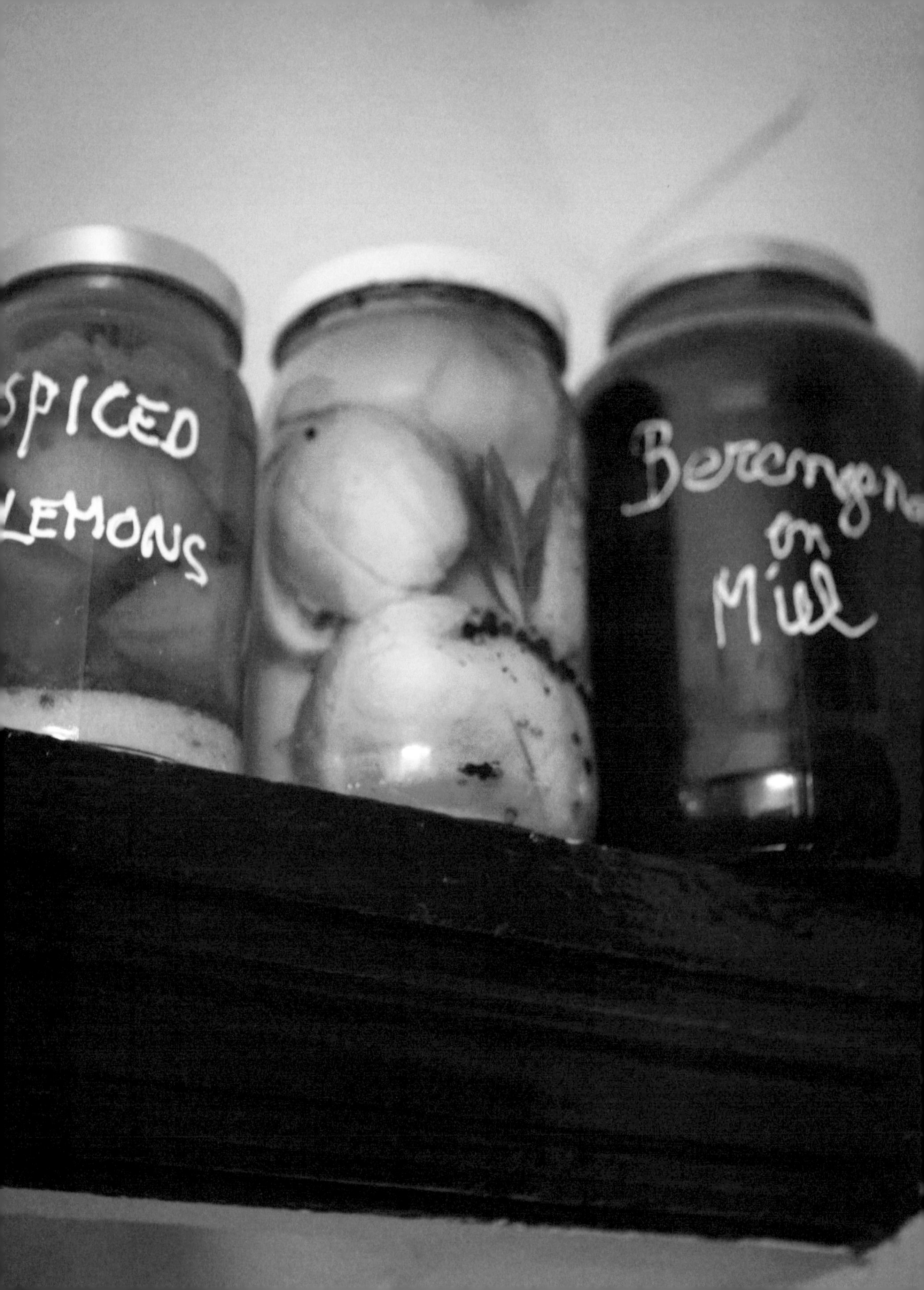
SPICED
LEMONS
Miel

⬩ Skim off the froth, allow to cool, and bottle into several sterilised wide-mouthed 1 litre (1¾ pint) preserving jars (see page 198). When cool, cover with a layer of olive oil, making certain that none of the aubergines sticks out above it. Store the jar in a cool larder.

⬩ They will keep for up to a year, but you will probably have eaten them well before that!

Preserved lemons in oil

Makes 1 litre (1¾ pint) jar

3–6 organic unwaxed lemons (thin-skinned varieties are best), or as many as you can get into the jar without having to ram them in too tightly

sea salt

1 cinnamon stick

4–5 bay leaves

small handful of peppercorns

sunflower oil

olive oil

I make only a few of these lemons at a time as we only use the thinnest strips of lemon peel in some of our dishes and, if you don't use them up, they lose their charm after six months or so. If you are going to use a lot of preserved lemons, double the recipe. I prefer to make a new batch every few months, so we have them to hand and they are still yellow. After a few months they will bleach out to a whitish colour, but the oil will have become more lemony.

⬩ Have ready a large bowl, such as a mixing bowl for bread making. Wash the lemons and dry them with a soft cloth.

⬩ Carefully cut the lemons by making three cross cuts in them lengthways, from the stalk end to the tip, but without cutting through the tip of the lemon so that the skin is still joined together.

⬩ Holding one of the lemons in your hand over the bowl, joined end down so that the lemon opens up like the petals of a flower, spoon 1 heaped tbsp of salt over the inside of the lemon, then press the 'petals' together and lay the lemon into the bowl on its side. Repeat with all the lemons.

⬩ Break the cinnamon stick in two. Pack the lemons into a 1 litre (1¾ pint) sterilised Kilner jar (see page 198). Stick the two sections of cinnamon stick into the jar, and post in the bay leaves and a few peppercorns. Cover with a mixture of sunflower oil and olive oil and close the lid firmly.

⬩ Keep this in the sunshine for a day or two, then put it away into a shady cool place.

cont...

⚜ These lemons will be ready for use in a couple of months. To use, remove a lemon with a slotted spoon, take off the segments required and rinse under a cold tap. Put the segments, skin side down, on a board, and scrape off and discard the softened flesh and pith. The salty zest is great, slivered finely, for flavouring meat tagines and chickpea salads.

Indian-style pickled lemons

Makes 3 x 1 litre (1¾ pint) jars

1 tbsp coriander seeds

6 cloves, plus more for the jars

2 garlic cloves

1 tsp cardamom seeds

12–18 organic unwaxed lemons (thin-skinned varieties are best), or as many as you can get into the jar without having to ram them in too tightly, plus about 12 more lemons for juice

sea salt

1 cinnamon stick

4–5 bay leaves

small handful of peppercorns

sunflower oil

olive oil

These are cut up and salted in the same way as the lemons in the previous recipe, but are preserved in lemon juice. You will want to make a larger quantity of them than of the lemons in oil, as they are spooned on to plates to accompany curries.

⚜ Put the coriander seeds in a small dry frying pan with the cloves and garlic cloves. Place over a medium heat and stir until the whole smells fragrant. Mix with the cardamom in a mortar and grind to a paste with the pestle. Mix in the juice of eight lemons, stir, then allow to macerate for one hour.

⚜ Cut the whole lemons and rub in the salt, as in the previous recipe. Close the 'petals' of the fruit over the salty centres, and pack between three sterilised 1 litre (1¾ pint) jars (see page 198), with 2 cloves in each as well as a shard of cinnamon, some bay leaves and peppercorns. Pour over the spiced lemon juice. If you haven't quite got enough juice to cover the lemons, squeeze a few more, adding juice until the jar is almost filled.

⚜ Float a thin layer of sunflower and olive oils on top to seal. Leave the jars in a cool storecupboard for four to six months. They are mighty sour, but excellent with curries.

Lemon oil

Makes 600ml (1 pint)

7 organic (unwaxed) lemons

1 tsp cumin seeds

400ml (14fl oz) sunflower oil

200ml (7fl oz) olive oil

I like to use a dash of this oil when I am making a lemon mayonnaise for white fish, or sometimes use it to help along preserved lemon zest when I am making Moroccan chicken with olives and preserved lemon (see page 117). The oil is also lovely poured over boiled green haricot beans, but not on its own as the scent can be too powerful, just use a dash mixed with vinaigrette. You can dot around some string-thin slices of preserved lemon zest and thin slices of onion.

◖ Wash the lemons and zest them finely with a zester or sharp knife so that you do not get any of the pith.

◖ Put the lemon zest into a clear sterilised bottle (see page 198) with the cumin seeds and cover with the oils.

◖ Leave the bottle in the sunshine for one week, then move to a cold larder for two more weeks before using. Strain the oil and pour into a fresh sterilised bottle to store.

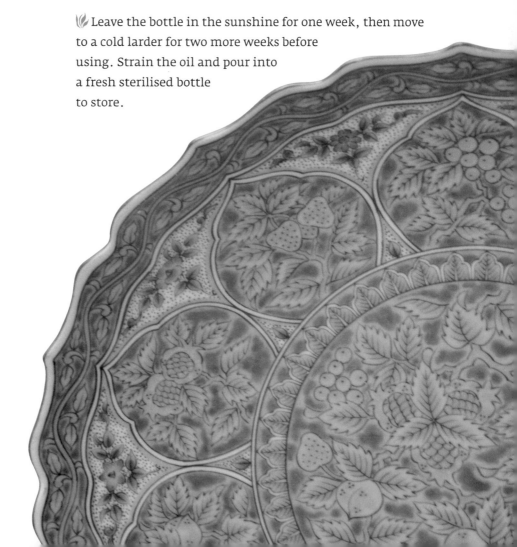

Tomato and cardamom jam

Makes 12 or more 340g (12oz) jam pots

3.6kg (8lb) tomatoes, skinned and deseeded (see page 96)

3.6kg (8lb) granulated sugar

juice and finely grated zest of 6 unwaxed lemons

2 tsp finely ground cardamom seeds

This recipe comes from Nathalie Hambro's *Particular Delights*, published by Jill Norman in 1981. A book full of inspiration.

The delicately spiced jam is delicious with a slice of manchego cheese or with hot cheese soufflés or grilled goat's cheese. We often spoon a little around Goat's cheese, aubergine and tomato pesto stacks (see page 41). It is strong and exotic, the perfect marriage of Eastern spice with tomatoes from the New World.

It is also excellent served with monkfish or bacalao, either as it comes or stirred into mayonnaise. And on toast for breakfast!

There is a lot of sugar in this, in order to make the tomatoes almost candied in their own syrup. This is combated by the juice of the lemons and the innate acidity of the tomatoes themselves.

Put the tomatoes in a preserving pan with the sugar, stir and leave to stand overnight or for at least three hours before cooking, so the sugar dissolves. (To hasten the process you can put in a layer of tomatoes, then one of sugar, another of tomatoes and so on.)

When you are ready to cook, add the lemon juice and zest and the cardamom and bring to the boil. Skim the foam from the top from time to time. Have ready 12 or more 340g (12oz) sterilised jam pots (see page 198) which have been gently heated in the oven or on top of the stove. Test the jam for a set: just take 1 tsp of the hot mixture and drop it on to a cold plate. Wait half a minute, tilt the plate to see if the jam runs (if it does it will need further cooking straight away). If it looks firm, then wait until the jam is cool, then rub your finger through it to see if the streak which you leave in the middle of the jam stays there, with each jammy side remaining separate. There should also be signs of some wrinkling on the surface of the jam. This means it has set. The pectin in the lemon juice should help this to happen fairly swiftly.

Let it cool for a few minutes then, with a funnel and ladle, fill the pots, cover and label. Your jam should be completely translucent.

Preserved anchovies in oil

Whenever you find good fresh anchovies – in Spain, early spring to summer is the best bet – rush them home, decapitate them and rinse them under a cold tap, at the same time whip out the guts and the backbone with your thumb.

❧ Put them in a bowl with sea salt, bay leaves and chopped chillies. Leave overnight somewhere cool, covered with cling film.

❧ Next day, tip out any liquid and pack the anchovies into sterilised jam jars (see page 198). I like to put them in vertically, sprinkling sea salt over them all the while, until they are packed fairly tightly. Poke some red chillies into the jar, with one bay leaf, cut into strips. Cover with olive oil and put the lid on.

❧ Keep them for two months before using them. They're excellent and will keep for up to one year.

❧ When you want to use them, pick out the fillets required, soak in water for five minutes, then press dry before eating them on toast, or adding them to roast lamb, pasta sauce, or anchoïade. Or make anchovy butter, or aubergine and anchovy caviar, or even bagna cauda, the Piedmontese hot dip made from olive oil, butter, crushed walnuts, garlic and anchovy. It's the perfect dip for crudités.

Carne de membrillo
Quince cheese

equal quantities of quince and granulated sugar

juice of 1–2 lemons, about 250ml (9fl oz) of juice, depending on the size of the lemons, plus more if needed

a little sunflower oil (optional)

a little icing sugar (optional)

The heady perfume of quinces is only fully released when they are cooked. This fruit paste can be dried in the oven, cut into squares and dusted with icing sugar, when it is served as a sweetmeat with coffee; or it may be left as it is to set in a tupperware bowl and, when cool, turned out on to a board and sliced. In this case it is the perfect accompaniment for cheese.

It makes no sense to stipulate quantities here, as we work with what we can harvest, while you, dear reader, might be constrained by the price of quinces in your neck of the woods.

Core the quinces but do not peel them. Remove any imperfections. Chop them and place in a preserving pan with the lemon juice, then cook over a medium heat until the fruit is soft. Do not add any additional liquid as the fruit will make its own.

Add the sugar and allow to dissolve over a gentle heat. If it does not dissolve, add 1–2 tbsp of water. Cook the fruit and sugar together without burning. The fruit pulp should turn a glorious old rose colour. Purée in the pan with a hand-held blender, stir and taste when a little cool. If the paste seems too sweet to you, add the juice of another lemon.

To make fruit jellies, pour the paste into shallow, oiled oven dishes and allow it to dry gently for a day or two in a slow Aga. If you don't have one, then leave them in a warm dry place such as an airing cupboard for one week. When dried to a tough gelatinous consistency, turn the slab of jelly out on to greaseproof paper, slice into diamonds and sprinkle with icing sugar. These will keep in an airtight tin. They sometimes give out a little syrup but, when you want to serve them, just dust them again with icing sugar and put on a plate to go out with coffee after dinner.

It's more usual to use the purée as regular *carne de membrillo*. Pour the purée out immediately it is slightly cooled into a tupperware bowl or box. Let it get cold, then refrigerate. When you want to use it, tip it out as a block on a side plate and put on the table at the same time as the cheese board, with a knife beside it for slicing off slivers or chunks, according to taste.

Basil oil

Gather sprigs of basil from the garden, well before the basil goes to flower, but when it has already acquired luxuriant foliage. Rinse off any dust under a cold tap, but make sure the leaves are completely dry or they will rot in the oil.

🌿 Mix 800ml (1 pint 7fl oz) of sunflower oil with 200ml (7fl oz) of olive oil. Pack the basil sprigs into a 1-litre (1¾ pint) sterilised Kilner jar (see page 198). Cover with the mixture of oils, making sure all the leaves are submerged. Screw on the lid tightly, or clip on the rubber-flanged lid if that is the type of jar you have.

🌿 Stand for four or five days (and up to a maximum of one week) in strong sunlight, then remove the basil, which will have gone slimy, and discard.

🌿 Tip the oil into a sterilised glass bottle (see page 198) and cork firmly. Use on winter salads when you want to bring back the flavour of summer.

Spicy tomato ketchup

Makes about 400ml (14fl oz)

1kg (2lb 4oz) cherry tomatoes

5 red chillies, chopped, seeds left in

2 large sweet white onions, peeled and chopped

1kg (2lb 4oz) granulated sugar

5 cloves

1 tsp ground cardamom seeds

salt, to taste

1 litre (1¾ pints) strong white wine vinegar

We use the smallest of our tomatoes for this, as they are a nuisance for anything else. If there is a glut of cherry tomatoes, we rip up the plants at the end of the season and strip the bunches of fruit from their stems. It's best to put them in a plastic fruit crate out in the yard, then hose them down to get rid of any particles of earth or leaves and grass. Let them drip dry before you bring the crate into the kitchen!

You will probably want to make much more than the bottle or so this recipe makes, so just scale up all the quantities.

The simplest way is to process the tomatoes, chillies and onions in my Magimix coulis maker! The machine is quick and its centrifuge throws out the juice and the pulp and keeps back seeds and skins. Alternatively, push them through a vegetable mouli, but this takes longer. If you have a food processor, then another way is to liquidise the vegetables, then pass them through a nylon sieve into a saucepan, working at the pulp with a wooden spoon and leaving the pips and skins behind. (You will need to stop every now and then to clear the sieve of debris.) Here, these scrapings go straight into the bucket of scraps for the chickens. You could put them on the compost heap, if you don't object to a sudden spurt of cherry tomato plants sprouting there next summer!

To the pulp, add the sugar, spices, salt and vinegar and put the pan over a low heat. Let it simmer for several hours, skimming off the scum as you go, until it has reduced by half. When it has reached the consistency of ketchup, it will be spitting like porridge. Remove it from the heat before you have to redecorate the kitchen entirely and bottle it into sterilised old-fashioned screw-top cider or beer bottles (see page 198). If you have not got these, use ordinary wine bottles and seal them with a cork-based stopper from a sherry or port bottle. Store in a cool larder.

This ketchup will keep well for a year or so, but we use it up quite quickly as an ingredient for our marinade for Barbecued Iberian pork ribs (see right).

Barbecued Iberian pork ribs

Mix 5 large tbsp ketchup, 1 large tbsp soy sauce, and ½ tsp smoked hot paprika (*pimientón picante de la Vera*) with 3 crushed garlic cloves and 125ml (4fl oz) of olive oil. For four to five people you will need 20 ribs, cut in half; we use Iberian pork ribs. To remove the surplus fat, boil the ribs in water, then skim the fat from the water. Extract the ribs with a slotted spoon. Salt them, then put them into the bowl of marinade. Stir them around with your hand, cover and leave to marinate for one hour, then grill them on the barbecue.

Bottled tomatoes

Larger beef tomatoes and plum tomatoes are good for bottling. They last all year and mean we can have fresh-tasting summer-ripe tomatoes even in winter.

❦ We put the whole tomatoes in a pan, pour on boiling water and, after five minutes, skin them (the skins just slip off).

❦ Place some narrow- or wide-necked sterilised fruit juice jars (see page 198) into a flat plastic laundry bowl, then force the tomatoes into them with the handle of a wooden spoon (see photo, left). Cut them into quarters if necessary. You want to avoid having air pockets in the jar if possible, and you will soon discover why it's important to have the jars sitting in a wide basin when you do this, as the juice goes everywhere.

❦ When you have filled 12 x 1-litre (1¾ pint) bottles, place them in a very large, deep pan. Loosely screw on the tops, then pour water into the pan up to the necks of the bottles. Bring to the boil and simmer for 30–45 minutes. Turn off the heat and leave the bottles to cool slowly in the pan. Tighten the screw tops and, as they cool, the jars will become vacuum sealed.

❦ Any spare juice makes very good Bloody Marys with the addition of salt, Tabasco, lemon juice and fino before the vodka is added!

Sun-dried tomatoes

As our mountain tomatoes ripen too late in the season to be sun-dried (the sun loses its greatest heat by mid-August), we generally buy in early beef tomatoes from the plains that are ripe when the weather in our hills is beginning to heat up, in late June and early July. The tomato prices have dropped by then, so it's worth the investment.

🌿 We pull them off the stalks and cut them in two across their equators so the core is in the middle and the chambers radiate out from it. We sprinkle them with sea salt and place them, face up, on trays lined with foil, shiny side up.

🌿 The trays go on to the roof terrace outside our bedroom, and the tomatoes are ready in three or four days if the weather is hot and dry. It's important to bring the trays in at night, in case the temperature drops enough for it to approach dew point. (If you don't do this, the salt will attract any humidity in the air and the tomatoes will start to turn mouldy.)

🌿 When the tomatoes are dry enough, still soft and bendy but not yet hard and cardboardy, pack them into jam jars and cover with sunflower oil. Store in a cool larder. These will last all year, and are excellent for making Sun-dried tomato pesto (see page 33), or for throwing into winter casseroles which need that tomato kick.

Searching though our larder and storecupboard we now have the ingredients to hand for a sun-dried tomato pesto, a tapenade, houmous, an anchoïade, pasta with caper and tomato sauce... in short, the surprise visitor will not catch us on the wrong foot. We can knock up a toast with fresh goat's cheese and anchovy, or goat's cheese with honey and oregano. We can whisk quince cheese into a bowl of mayonnaise to make Quince alioli (see page 32), so delicious with cold leftover roast lamb. We can slice a chorizo finely, and have triangles of manchego cheese with a dollop of Quince cheese, Tomato and cardamom jam, or Aubergines candied in honey (see pages 210, 208 and 202). We can cut up a beef tomato and sprinkle it with sea salt and dried oregano leaves... the lovely possibilities go on and on.

A guide for American cooks

LIQUID MEASURE CONVERSIONS
METRIC ➠ IMPERIAL ➠ US MEASURE

30ml ≈ 1fl oz ≈ ⅛ cup

60ml ≈ 2fl oz ≈ ¼ cup

120ml ≈ 4fl oz ≈ ½ cup

240ml ≈ 8fl oz ≈ 1 cup

480ml ≈ 16fl oz ≈ 1 US pint

600ml ≈ 1 UK pint ≈ 1 US pint plus ½ cup

DRY MEASURE CONVERSIONS
US MEASURE ➠ UK MEASURE

1 stick of butter ≈ 115g (4oz)

1 cup grated cheese ≈ 115g (4oz)

1 cup all-purpose flour ≈ 150g (5½oz)

1 cup superfine or granulated sugar ≈ 225g (8oz)

1 cup confectioner's sugar ≈ 140g (5oz)

1 cup ground almonds ≈ 115g (4oz)

1 cup raw rice ≈ 200g (7oz)

1 cup dried beans ≈ 225g (8oz)

1 cup canned beans (drained) ≈ 250g (9oz)

1 cup whole nuts ≈ 140g (5oz)

Index

Acknowledgements

I would like to thank the following people without whom this book would not have been possible.

IN MY KITCHEN
Pepi García Calero who keeps my kitchen spotless and orderly, and has looked after us for 25 years now. "Gracias por tu amistad, y por todo tu trabajo, Pepi, por habernos tanto ayudado y por tu paciencia, y tu presencia, siempre sonriendo."

IN MY HOUSE
Working on this book reminded Sam and me of the happy years spent watching you grow up, Charlie, Grania, and Jago. Thanks for being here.

IN OUR SPANISH BEGINNINGS
The Scott family of Trasierra, who taught us it was possible to make life into an adventure.

We sorely miss Pepín and Carmen Ybarra who, 30 years ago, introduced us to the Sierra de Aracena. They showed us the magic of this place.

WITH THE BOOK
Francine Lawrence for giving us the courage to approach an agent; Heather Holden-Brown, of HHB Literary Agency, who has been steadfast and calm throughout and full of wise advice; Anthony Weldon of Bene Factum Publishing who was brave and generous enough to take on the project; Lucy Bannell for her meticulous editing (any faults are surely mine), good humour and patience; Nicola Bailey for her clear design and layout and feeling for this project; Karen Howes for introducing us to Nicola, helping us through a mid-project crisis.

Very special thanks to Tim Clinch for his wonderful photographs, and for nagging us to write the book. Thanks too to Bill Bennett of Denman Bennett in Charleston SC, for allowing us to reproduce his photo of our sly smiling pig! Thank you Tommi Miers for your kind words and a big thank you to Darina Allen, for your energy and commitment to honesty in the kitchen and the kitchen garden which are an example to us all. We fondly remember a surfeit of roast duck, hidden away in magic West Cork and a long summer evening of chat among the fuchsia hedges.

IN CASTAÑUELO
María José Sevilla, huge thanks for the inspiration and the discussions we have had about ingredients, and for food, wine and laughter shared in these mountains. We remember those summer evenings in the magical fruit-filled valley where you hide in Spain. *Gambones* brushed with garlic and grilled, white wine from Victoria Parente in the Rueda, perfect figs, warm from the sun.

IN JEREZ
A big hug and a clinking of glasses with Gonzalo del Río González-Gordon, with whom we have spent many hours learning about sherry and it's unique qualities. Many thanks to your family for guidance, friendship and generous quantities of liquid amber from the Gonzalez Byass Bodegas. We remember the fun of the feria; the white-jacketed waiters, the frosty glasses of Tio Pepe, the fans, the flamenco dresses and the splendid cast-iron pavilion where we danced ourselves silly.

IN MAZAGÓN
The happy Caballero family, who keep us young in heart and longing to be grandparents. They understand sea, sun, sand, family life, the pleasures of *comida de cuchara*, and make excellent Lustau wines. From their wooden deck we have looked out over the tops of the pines, watched the sun setting in the Atlantic ocean and sipped Papirusa manzanilla as we ate little fried anchovies and other delights.

IN ARACENA
Thanks to Meli and Juanjo, and Blas and Flori who supplied us with vittles and gave us credit through the lean months of the early years.

Recommendations for Finca Buenvino
www.fincabuenvino.com

ON THE FARM

Thank you Rafa for growing wonderful organic vegetables. Thanks too, to Simon, who started the garden before walking with Rociera (a donkey) to Italy.

Last but not least, I would never have been able to raise three country-wild children AND cook for guests without a stream of English-speaking helpers from Europe, New Zealand, Australia and South Africa. Thank you, Jane, Caro, Murray and Julie, Pete, Jo and Harvey, Matty, Linda, Graham and Karen, Andrea, Steph, Nick and Carmen, Stevie, Robin, Che, Matthew, Raina (from the Cook Islands), Jeremy, Trent, Trevor and Jackie, Paula, Tina and years ago, Charlene and Gill, "Lord" Malcolm and, way back, the London double decker bus with the 'gentlemen's club' which contained a character from Broome called "H for harassment" and Donna and Linette in the old VW...

Lost in the mists of time are fearsome renditions of the Haka, cars rolled in the ditch, lamb roasted in a hangi; people who went missing at local fiestas, and new kitchen vocabulary. Anyone know what a 'fly disappointer' is?

We love you and will never forget the girl with 'reddy blacky spiky hair' who used to shout "Get to bed you little f•cker!" to our son, aged three, when he wanted to join the party long after bedtime.

I could not imagine Aracena without Jeannie and Sam or without Buenvino, their farm, located at the heart of the Sierra de Aracena nature park, one of the best-kept secrets in western Andalusia.

Life starts early at Buenvino and breakfast is an important part of the day. Rich home-made yogurt, jam, marmalade and bread baked by Jeannie the same morning or perhaps the night before. Eggs and bacon with truly ripe tomatoes and local morcilla or ham are cooked to order. Fresh fruit never comes from far: pomegranates and quinces in the winter and in the summer, dark and green figs and plums, apricots or peaches are always present at the Chesterton's table.

But it is at dinner that Buenvino truly comes alive, especially in the summer when, in the early evening, a glass or two of chilled sherry are served with *tapitas* of ham and locally marinated olives, chickpea cream and *montaditos*. Whilst you are admiring the roses and the geraniums, the large aviary and the magnificent view of the Sierras through the branches of a chestnut tree, dinner arrives announced by Jeannie. Who could resist a plate of minute clams cooked in butter and wine or another of fresh figs, goat's cheese and honey, or a refreshing courgette cream followed by roasted quail or the best tuna money can buy? These are just some of the great dishes I had the last time we were together, accompanied all along by laughter and friendship.

At Buenvino, food reflects the background of a creative and dedicated cook who understands what cooking with plenty of taste, colour and flair is all about.

MARÍA JOSÉ SEVILLA SALVADOR, FOODS & WINES FROM SPAIN, SPANISH TRADE COMMISSION, LONDON

Spending time at Buenvino with Sam and Jeannie is like a suspension of normal life. Time stands still whilst you eat amongst quince trees and the sounds of the forest, deep in the heart of pata negra pig country. Jeannie's delicious, restaurant-standard food abounds and wine flows freely; they live a life of comforting generosity and a general feeling of joie de vivre pervades the surrounding hills. I can't wait to buy this book and be transported back to their little corner of paradise.

THOMASINA MIERS, FOUNDER OF WAHACA RESTAURANTS

Every now and then I come across a really special place, a gem so out of the ordinary that I have mixed feelings about revealing its whereabouts... We arrived close to midnight, almost too tired to eat, but the warm and spontaneous welcome revived us. A huge fire crackled on the hearth in the drawing room. We had a delicious soup with homemade breads and Spanish farmhouse cheeses: cabrales, manchego, a creamy melting torta wrapped in its traditional band of lace and the famous tetilla. In the morning, the view across the hills, thickly wooded with sweet chestnut and cork oak, was spectacular. Breakfast was thick unctuous home-made yogurt, local honey and crunchy granola, dried fruit, home-made jam and Seville orange marmalade, lots of hot toast, bacon, and eggs from their own hens.

DARINA ALLEN,
THE IRISH EXAMINER

Jeannie draws upon local ingredients such as sherry, pork, and the wild mushrooms found in the countryside. Judging by the meal she served on the evening we visited: pasta with scallops and sun-dried tomatoes; tender Iberian black pig with wild mushrooms; beetroot rice; and a cream cheese dessert with raspberry coulis, Jeannie is a force to be reckoned with in the kitchen.

COGNOSCENTI INTERNET MAGAZINE, NEW YORK

Here we enjoyed walking among rolling cork and chestnut woods before sitting down to a magnificent dinner of home-cured ham, home-made black pudding and a roasted fillet from the home-bred pig, killed at the *matanza* the week before. We were woken in our gorgeous bedroom by the smell of wood smoke and coffee.

TREVOR GROVE,
THE DAILY TELEGRAPH

Had I stumbled into a Rosamund Pilcher novel? At breakfast, the sun streamed in through the window of the panelled dining room, where pots of basil adorned the long table. The delicious jams were made with fruit from nearby trees, and the yogurt from the milk of goats that roam the estate. The aroma of bacon wafted from the kitchen. Pots of steaming coffee... well, I think you've got the idea by now.

The previous evening we had gathered in the comfy drawing-room for drinks and tapas – which, of course, included ham from pigs reared on the estate. We later drifted into the conservatory, where a paella was served to the diners, some were guests, others neighbours, or friends just passing through.

ANNIE BENNETT,
THE DAILY TELEGRAPH

Sam and Jeannie have created a congenial, Woosterish country-house party in the mountains of western Andalusia. Their palacio has a pool terrace for soaking up silence and a communal lounge ideal for taking on liberal quantities of sherry and swapping tales with fellow guests. The Chestertons were recently adopted as members of their nearest village; Jeannie shares her knowledge of Andalusian cuisine on regular courses; and Sam's the man for guidance on the Sierra de Aracena's walking trails. Pack stiff boots and expect stiff gins.

THE SUNDAY TIMES: OUR 20 TOP CONTINENTAL HOTELS

I went high up in the mountains of Andalusia to the beautiful, comforting home – Finca Buenvino – of Sam and Jeannie Chesterton, for their week-long cookery course. It all takes place in the Chestertons' house. You sleep there, eat there and cook there, round Jeannie's kitchen table. Included in the trip is a day out to Jerez to drink sherry and eat, and trips into the local pretty towns. We went to a jamón festival but the finca also produces its own ham, chestnuts, olives and scented honey.

LUCY CAVENDISH, THE OBSERVER,
TOP TEN COOKERY COURSES.

North from Seville, hidden among woodlands in which nightingales sing, Finca Buenvino is a family home as much as it is a hotel. The family in question belong to Jeannie and Sam Chesterton, expats who have created a truly mouthwatering retreat in the heart of Andalusia. There are five rooms in the main house, plus several self-catering cottages. Dinner, preceded by home-made tapas, is served on the long table in the main house. Jeannie is a Cordon Bleu cook who shares her skills with the guests who arrive every summer for residential cookery courses.

There's a stunning lagoon swimming pool with a view of the hills, and a pool house, complete with bedroom, to go with it. Wild boar and genet cat among other elusive creatures are seen in the nature reserve, and there's a cottage there, too. The main house is a family home. It was built by the Chestertons themselves using materials salvaged from old buildings in the area. In winter, log fires and afternoon high teas keep out the cold; in summer, the estate is carpeted in wild flowers. Walking, mountain biking or riding through the surrounding countryside, or visiting local village fiestas, are the principal activities.

TRAVEL INTELLIGENCE

The Finca stands in the heart of the Sierra de Aracena National Park which comprises thousands of hectares of cork oak and sweet chestnut forests: the oaks also provide acorns for the fabulous hams for which the area is world-famous. It is one of the most peaceful and tranquil places on earth. The view from the terrace is breathtaking, looking across the mountains to the occasional white village beyond. At night the unpolluted skies offer views of the stars such as you will never see in England.

Jeannie is an outstanding cook, and the food alone offers a good reason to come. Most of the produce is grown on the estate. Dinner is served outdoors in summer (or in their beautiful dining room if it is cool). Jeannie organises occasional cookery weekends; Sam keeps an excellent cellar.

Guest rooms are spacious and delightfully furnished, with very comfortable beds and the softest of pillows; all have extensive collections of books to borrow. Breakfast is one of life's pleasures: freshly squeezed orange juice, fruit, home-made muesli, local yogurt, home-made bread and jams, bacon and eggs (the eggs are of course from the estate), all served on the terrace looking out at that view.

To work up an appetite I habitually go for a two-mile walk before breakfast down the track to the vegetable garden (*huerta*) where Sam has three cottages, each with its own plunge pool. This morning I encountered three wild deer, and helped myself to a few of the first figs of the season. It soon gets too hot to take strenuous exercise (those who disagree may borrow mountain bikes). Fortunately the Finca has a wonderful open-air "infinity" (more spectacular mountain views) swimming pool where it is all too easy to spend the morning and afternoon.

CHRISTOPHER KIRKER'S TRAVEL BLOG, *MR AND MRS KIRKER*

First published in 2014 by
Bene Factum Publishing Ltd
PO Box 58122
London
SW8 5WZ

EMAIL inquiries@bene-factum.co.uk
www.bene-factum.co.uk

ISBN 978-1-909657-29-8

Text copyright © Sam and Jeannie Chesterton, 2013

A CIP catalogue record for this book is available from the British Library.

Designer Nicola Bailey
Editor Lucy Bannell

Printed in China for Latitude Press

PICTURE CREDITS

All images by Tim Clinch except:
Page 119 (pigs), by Bill Bennett/
Denman Bennett Images)
Additional photography by Nicola Bailey